Lincolnshire
and the Wolds

W A L K S

Compiled by
Brian Conduit

JARROLD
publishing

Acknowledgements
My thanks for the valuable advice and numerous useful
leaflets that I obtained from the various tourist information
centres throughout Lincolnshire.

Text: Brian Conduit
Photography: Brian Conduit
Editor: Geoffrey Sutton
Designer: Doug Whitworth

Series Consultant: Brian Conduit

Ordnance Survey This product includes mapping data licensed
from Ordnance Survey® with the permission
of the Controller of Her Majesty's Stationery Office. © Crown
Copyright 2002. All rights reserved. Licence number 100017593.
Pathfinder is a registered trade mark of Ordnance Survey, the
national mapping agency of Great Britain.

Jarrold Publishing   ISBN 978-0-7117-2082-4

First published 2002 by Jarrold Publishing
This edition printed for The Book People 2007.

Printed in Singapore. BP1/07

Jarrold Publishing
Pathfinder Guides, Whitefriars, Norwich NR3 1TR
E-mail: pathfinder@jarrold.com
www.jarrold-publishing.co.uk/pathfinders

Front cover: The gatehouse of ruined Thornton Abbey
Previous page: The two churches of Alvingham

Contents

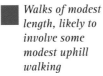

■ Short, easy walks

■ Walks of modest length, likely to involve some modest uphill walking

■ More challenging walks which may be longer and/or over more rugged terrain, often with some stiff climbs

Keymap 1

Keymap 1

SCALE 1:333 333 or 1 INCH to about 5¼ MILES *1CM to 3.3KM*

KEYMAP HEIGHTS SHOWN IN FEET

HORNCASTLE
SPILSBY
SKEGNESS
Wainfleet All Saints
Wainfleet St Mary
Wainfleet Sand
Friskney
Friskney Flats
Coningsby
Tattershall
Stickney
Sibsey
Old Leake
Wrangle
Leverton
Benington
BOSTON
Butterwick Low
Roger Sand
THE W
Toft Sand
Gat Sand
Black Buoy Sand
Mare Tail
Old South
Old Lynn Channel
Long Sand
Breast Sand
BOSTON DEE
Kirton
Wyberton
Frampton
Swineshead
Donington
Sutterton
Fosdyke
Gosberton
Pinchbeck
SPALDING
Moulton
Whaplode
HOLBEACH
Holbeach Marsh
Gedney Marsh
Long Sutton
Sutton Bridge
Terrington St Clement
Terrington Marsh
Tydd St Giles
WISBECH
Leverington
Crowland
Thorney
PETERBOROUGH
WHITTLESEY
MARCH
Outwell
Welney
Upwell Fen
Marshland Fen
Bedford Level (North Level)
A16
A17
A52
A151
A158
A1101
A47
A15
SCALE 1:333 333 or 1 INCH to about 5¼ MILES 1CM to 3.3KM
0 2 4 6 8 10 KILOMETRES 15
0 2 4 6 MILES 8 10
KEYMAP HEIGHTS SHOWN IN FEET

At-a-glance...

Walk	Page	Start	Nat. Grid Reference	Distance	Time
Alvingham and the Louth Canal	14	Alvingham Mill	TF 366914	3½ miles (5.6km)	1½ hrs
Around Horncastle	74	Horncastle	TF 259696	9 miles (14.5km)	4½ hrs
Barnetby le Wold, Bigby and Somerby	71	Barnetby le Wold	TA 056098	7½ miles (12.1km)	3½ hrs
Barton and the River Humber	24	Barton Waterside, Clay Pits car park	TA 027235	5½ miles (8.9km)	2½ hrs
Boston and the River Witham	34	Market Place, Boston	TF 327442	6½ miles (10.5km)	3 hrs
Bourne Wood and Edenham	50	Bourne	TF 096202	6½ miles (10.5km)	3 hrs
Chapel St Leonards, Hogsthorpe and Chapel Point	53	Chapel St Leonards	TF 561723	7 miles (11.3km)	3½ hrs
Claythorpe Mill and the Swaby valley	28	Aby village hall	TF 412784	5½ miles (8.9km)	2½ hrs
Crowland and the River Welland	68	Crowland	TF 239103	8½ miles (13.7km)	4 hrs
Donington and the Bain valley	44	Donington on Bain	TF 235830	6 miles (9.7km)	3 hrs
Four Lincoln Edge villages	87	Wellingore	SK 983566	9 miles (14.5km)	4½ hrs
Isle of Axholme	37	Epworth, Church Walk car park	SE 784039	6½ miles (10.5km)	3 hrs
Laceby, Irby Upon Humber and Aylesby	84	Laceby	TA 214065	8 miles (12.9km)	4 hrs
Lincoln and the Fossdyke	59	Castle Hill, Lincoln	SK 976718	7½ miles (12.1km)	3½ hrs
Long Sutton and South Holland Main Drain	62	Long Sutton	TF 432228	7½ miles (12.1km)	3½ hrs
North Carlton and Scampton	22	Till Bridge Lane Viewpoint, A1500/B1398	SK 954784	4½ miles (7.2km)	2 hrs
Old Bolingbroke and East Keal	56	Old Bolingbroke	TF 349652	6½ miles (10.5km)	3½ hrs
Sea banks of the Wash	40	Moulton Marsh Nature Reserve	TF 343335	6½ miles (10.5km)	3 hrs
Southrey, Bardney and Tupholme Abbey	65	Ferry Road, Southrey	TF 138664	8½ miles (13.7km)	4 hrs
Spalding	20	Ayscoughfee Hall Gardens, Spalding	TF 249224	4½ miles (7.2km)	2 hrs
Stamford, Easton on the Hill and Tinwell	31	Red Lion Square, Stamford	SK 028072	5½ miles (8.9km)	2½ hrs
Tattershall and Coningsby	16	Tattershall	TF 213578	3½ miles (5.6km)	1½ hrs
Tealby and Kirmond le Mire	81	Tealby	TF 157908	7 miles (11.3km)	3½ hrs
Tennyson Country	26	Tetford	TF 333748	5 miles (8km)	2½ hrs
Thornton Abbey	18	Thornton Abbey	TA 115190	3½ miles (5.6km)	1½ hrs
Vale of Belvoir	42	Woolsthorpe By Belvoir	SK 837342	6½ miles (10.5km)	3 hrs
Walesby, Claxby and Normanby le Wold	78	Walesby	TF 134924	6 miles (9.7km)	3 hrs
Woodhall Spa	47	Woodhall Spa	TF 193631	6½ miles (10.5km)	3 hrs

Comments

The walk starts by a picturesque mill and two adjacent churches and includes an attractive stretch beside the Louth Canal and fine views across reclaimed marshland.

The walk takes you across the countryside of the Bain valley near Horncastle, with an attractive and relaxing finale alongside the Horncastle Canal.

The open and sweeping views extend to Humberside on this fine walk in the northern wolds, which passes through two hamlets with medieval churches.

This varied walk starts by the Humber Bridge and includes a Saxon church, view of The Wolds and attractive walking beside the Humber estuary.

Three waterways – Maud Foster Drain, Frith Bank Drain and the River Witham – are used on this Fenland walk to the north of Boston. There are particularly memorable views of Boston Stump.

There is pleasant woodland walking with superb views over the valley of the East Glen River.

An opening walk across fields and reclaimed coastal marshes is followed by a final stretch along a sandy beach.

The route through pleasant wolds country passes a watermill, now a wildfowl garden, and takes you through the lovely, steep-sided Swaby valley.

The walk follows a lengthy stretch of the River Welland to the north of Crowland across a totally flat Fenland landscape.

The first part of the walk is above the Bain valley; the final stretch is beside the river. The views are superb throughout, even extending to Lincoln Cathedral.

There are superb views on this walk, the first half of which is mostly along the base of Lincoln Edge. The return is along the top, passing through four limestone villages.

This pleasant walk in the flat country of the Isle of Axholme starts in the attractive village where John and Charles Wesley were born.

Three attractive villages are linked on this outstanding walk in the northern wolds, not far from Grimsby and the Humber estuary.

Some of Lincoln's major historic sites are combined with a walk alongside the Fossdyke, originally cut by the Romans.

This walk across a wide and flat landscape includes one of Fenland's outstanding churches and a stretch beside South Holland Main Drain.

There are wide views across the Trent valley from Lincoln Edge at the start and end of the walk.

From the scanty remains of Bolingbroke Castle, the route heads up over the wolds to the village of East Keal. There are fine views over both Fens and coast.

There is a genuinely remote feel on this lonely and highly atmospheric walk above the marshes and creeks of the Wash.

This walk in the Witham valley includes two villages, woodland, monastic remains and a series of wide views.

A wholly waterside ramble, using the River Welland and Coronation Channel to create an interesting and satisfying walk around the attractive town of Spalding.

The walk links the historic town of Stamford with two attractive villages. There are fine views and beautiful riverside meadows.

This short walk is full of interest – two medieval churches, a castle, the Battle of Britain display and attractive walking beside the River Bain.

A walk across a typically rolling wolds landscape of gentle slopes and wide dry valleys, starting in an outstandingly attractive village.

This attractive walk in the heart of the Lincolnshire Wolds passes through the tiny hamlet where the great Victorian poet was born and lived for much of his early life.

On this circuit of the country around Thornton Abbey there are many views of the striking abbey ruins.

Main features of the walk are the wide vistas over the vale, attractive walking beside the Grantham Canal and the magnificent views of Belvoir Castle, seen from many different angles.

This is a classic walk over some of the highest and most scenic parts of the Lincolnshire Wolds, with the chance to visit the Ramblers' Church above Walesby.

An opening stretch across fields and along quiet lanes is followed by a delightful finale through some of the woodlands around Woodhall Spa.

At-a-glance...

Introduction to Lincolnshire and the Wolds

Lincolnshire is one of England's largest counties, second in size only to Yorkshire. Like Yorkshire it was traditionally divided into three areas: Lindsey in the north, Kesteven in the south-west and Holland in the south-east.

The usual response when telling someone that you are going to Lincolnshire is a dismissive comment about its flatness. A brief glance at some of the photographs in this guide will confirm that there is a lot more to the county. It does have hills that rise to over 540ft (165m) – but the belief that it mainly consists of flat landscapes is the commonest misconception. Just try walking up Steep Hill in Lincoln to the cathedral and castle and never again will you believe that Lincolnshire is flat.

Two main upland areas

In reality Lincolnshire comprises a lot of flat country broken up by two main upland areas, one long and narrow and the other shorter but wider. Perhaps the easiest way in which to understand its topography is to take an imaginary journey across it from west to east.

The western part of Lincolnshire is flat, extending from the Humber estuary in the north, through the Isle of Axholme and the Trent valley to the wide expanses of the Vale of Belvoir in the south.

Looking eastward, the western escarpment of Lincoln Edge (or Lincoln Cliff) is seen on the horizon, not a steep escarpment for the most part but nevertheless a significant physical feature. This is a long but narrow limestone ridge, part of the range of limestone uplands that extend north-eastwards across England from the Cotswolds, through south Warwickshire, Northamptonshire, Rutland and Lincolnshire, and on into Yorkshire. Here there are attractive old towns and villages built from the local stone, whose colouring varies from pale cream in some areas to darker orangey-brown ironstone at both the north and south ends. It is this ironstone that gave rise to the iron and steel industries of Scunthorpe in the north and Corby – just over the Northamptonshire border – in the south. Lincoln grew up where the River Witham cuts through this limestone ridge, and the towers of its hilltop cathedral dominate the city and much of the surrounding countryside, visible from over 20 miles (32km) away.

The Wolds – rolling countryside at its finest

To the east of Lincoln Edge stretches the clay vale of Lincoln Heath and beyond that are the Lincolnshire Wolds, the highest hills and arguably the most attractive countryside in the county. The Wolds are chalk hills, part of the series of chalk outcrops that extends roughly north-eastwards from the Chilterns, appearing at intervals in Cambridgeshire, continuing through Lincolnshire and reappearing on the other side of the Humber as the Yorkshire Wolds. This is rolling countryside at its finest, with slopes that range from gentle to moderately steep, wide dry valleys and panoramic views from the higher points over heath, marsh and fen. Among the many delightful villages scattered throughout the wolds is the tiny hamlet of Somersby, where Alfred Lord Tennyson was born, the son of the village rector.

The coast

Lastly on this west–east journey across the county there is the coastal strip running from the Humber to the Wash, partly reclaimed marshland and constantly vulnerable to the threat of invasion by the sea. It is a flat and fairly uniform coastline with virtually no cliffs, no estuaries and consequently no harbours between Grimsby on the Humber and Boston on the Wash. It is also a coastline of wide, sandy beaches – if inclined to be bracing as the legendary advertisement for Skegness states – and in the Victorian era, a string of holiday resorts grew up when rail links were created with the nearby industrial areas of Yorkshire and the East Midlands. A trip to Cleethorpes, Mablethorpe or 'Skeggy' became part of a way of life for many people in these areas, until at least the 1960s.

One area remains which does not fit into this west-east pattern but which no guide to the county can ignore. Most of south and south-east Lincolnshire comprises the vast, seemingly limitless expanses of the Fens, which extend across the county borders into neighbouring Cambridgeshire and Norfolk. Contrary to what some people say, these fenlands – and indeed the coastal marshlands, Isle of Axholme and the other flat landscapes of Lincolnshire – are not boring or featureless but have a unique appeal and a strange, haunting beauty. Wide skies, endless vistas, a sense of space and – certainly on the marshlands around the Wash – a feeling of remoteness and isolation can be experienced nowhere else in the region.

The Ramblers' Church, above Walesby

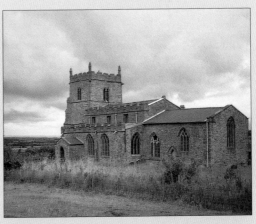

The Saxon church at Barton-Upon-Humber

Lincoln

Lincoln is the focal point of the county and has been so since Roman times. The Romans built a town here – Lindum Colonia – where the River Witham turns abruptly eastwards and cuts through the limestone ridge of Lincoln Edge to flow on to the sea. They also constructed the Fossdyke to link Lincoln to the Trent, still in existence and probably the earliest canal in the country. A few Roman remains survive in the city, notably the Newport Arch, one of only two surviving Roman gateways in England.

About 1,000 years after the Romans, the Norman conquerors built a castle and moved the seat of the diocese here. Both castle and cathedral are built on the site of the Roman fort and face each other on the highest part of the ridge. Lincoln Cathedral, a masterpiece of Gothic architecture, is regarded as one of the finest churches in Europe. Nearby are the ruins of the palace of the powerful medieval bishops, and on the steep downhill walk to the lower town you pass two of the earliest domestic buildings in the country – both dating from the 12th century. Spanning the Witham is the High Bridge, one of the few in England that still has buildings on it.

Stamford, Spalding and Boston

Lincolnshire has other historic towns, all well worth exploring. Stamford is a most appealing town, with a wealth of late-medieval churches and handsome houses, built from the local limestone. It is situated at the far south-western tip of the county, scarcely ½ mile (800m) from the borders of no less than three other counties – Cambridgeshire, Northamptonshire and Rutland. The views of its towers and spires from the water meadows adjoining the River Welland are particularly memorable.

Downstream along the Welland, Spalding is equally attractive but in a different way. This is a fenland town, with brick-built houses lining the river. It is the bulb capital of England and in springtime the town is a riot of colour.

Boston, situated at the mouth of the Witham, was once one of the most important ports in the country, and the great medieval church, noted for its strikingly tall tower, Boston Stump, is a reflection of its medieval prosperity. It was Puritans who emigrated from here to the New World in the 17th century who founded the town of Boston, Massachusetts.

Magnificent churches

A magnificent collection of churches is one of the chief glories of Lincolnshire. Particularly outstanding are the fenland churches, rivalled only by those of the Cotswolds, Somerset and East Anglia and mostly built from the profits of the wool trade. The list is a long one and everybody will have their personal favourites, but among the finest are those at Boston, Spalding, Long Sutton and Tattershall.

The Viking Way

The Viking Way is Lincolnshire's major long-distance footpath, snaking its way across the county from the south-west to the north. It runs along the ridge of Lincoln Edge to Lincoln, then heads across flat country beside the River Witham and Horncastle Canal to reach the wolds and continues over the wolds to end on the south side of the Humber Bridge. Many of the routes in this guide use stretches of the Viking Way to create a variety of circular walks.

An underrated walking area

As a walking area Lincolnshire is much underrated. There is a more varied landscape than many realise, paths are generally good and the standard of waymarking is among the best in the country.

Also, as most paths are not overused, they do not suffer from the erosion that is found in some other areas. Edge, heath, wolds, fen, coast and marsh – all are present in the following selection of walks which illustrates the rich diversity of a relatively little-known part of Britain.

View over the Bain valley

Alvingham and the Louth Canal

Start	Alvingham Mill
Distance	3½ miles (5.6km)
Approximate time	1½ hours
Parking	Alvingham Mill, by the 'Two Churches' sign
Refreshments	None
Ordnance Survey maps	Explorer 283 (Louth & Mablethorpe), Landranger 113 (Grimsby, Louth & Market Rasen)

The walk starts by a picturesque watermill and passes through a churchyard that contains two churches to reach the banks of the Louth Canal. It continues by the canal before heading off across reclaimed marshland to the village of North Cockerington and on to the start. The stretch beside the canal is most attractive, and there are immense views over the marshes, especially looking towards the coast.

Alvingham Mill was built in the 17th century, although there has been a mill on the site since the Middle Ages.

Begin by crossing the bridge by the mill, at a public footpath sign to Louth Canal, walk through a farmyard

Alvingham Mill

and go through a gate into a church-yard. Unusually, there are two adjacent medieval churches here. One was the parish church for Alvingham and the other – now redundant – served North Cockerington, although it is about ½ mile (800m) from the village. The latter may originally have been a

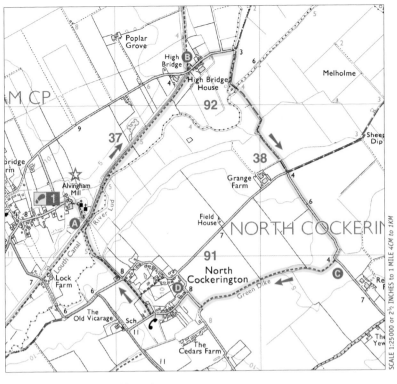

0 200 400 600 800 METRES 1 KILOMETRES
MILES
0 200 400 600 YARDS ½

chapel belonging to a nearby and now vanished priory.

Turn right along the right-hand edge of the churchyard, cross a footbridge over a ditch and keep ahead to cross a second footbridge over the Louth Canal Ⓐ. Turn left to walk along the embankment above the canal, built to provide a direct link between Louth and the North Sea coast. Climb a stile, keep ahead, and the path curves left to a stile by High Bridge.

Climb the stile, turn right Ⓑ along a lane and, where it ends, turn right, at a public bridleway sign, along an enclosed track. To the left, a solitary rock standing above the reclaimed marshes is topped by a triangulation pillar. At a fork in front of a cottage, take the left-hand track, cross a footbridge, go through a gate and walk along the right-hand edge of a field.

After crossing a channel, the path bends first left and then right, widens into a track and continues to a lane. Keep ahead along the narrow lane, follow it around a right-hand bend and, where it bends left Ⓒ, climb a stile and walk along a path above Green Dike on the left. Ahead in the distance the spire of Louth church and the line of the wolds can be seen. The path follows the curves of the dike to emerge, via a stile, onto a lane. Turn right into North Cockerington, take the first lane on the left Ⓓ and, at a public footpath sign, turn right along a hedge-lined track to a lane.

Cross over and take the path opposite – there is a fine view of Alvingham village and the two churches ahead – which winds across fields to reach the Louth Canal. Turn right alongside it and turn left over a bridge Ⓐ, here picking up the outward route, and retrace your steps to the start. ●

Tattershall and Coningsby

Start	Tattershall
Distance	3½ miles (5.6km)
Approximate time	1½ hours
Parking	Tattershall, off the Market Place
Refreshments	Pubs at Tattershall, pubs and café at Coningsby
Ordnance Survey maps	Explorer 261 (Boston), Landranger 122 (Skegness & Horncastle)

Although a short and flat walk, the considerable historic interest ranges from a redbrick 15th-century castle and two medieval churches to a Battle of Britain display. There is also pleasant walking beside the River Bain.

Tattershall is dominated by its castle and church, which rise majestically above the flat landscape. Both were built in the 15th century by Ralph, 3rd Lord Cromwell, who was Lord High Treasurer of England during the reign of Henry VI and one of the most powerful men in the country.

The dark, redbrick castle is a tall,

four-storied tower-house, which replaced a more modest earlier structure. After falling into disrepair, it was restored by Lord Curzon at the beginning of the 20th century and is now maintained by the National Trust.

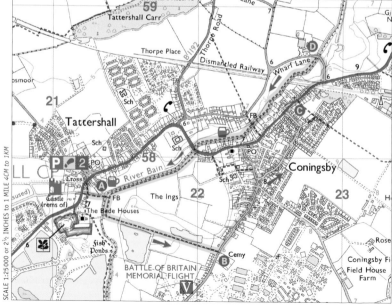

Tattershall church from the castle

The collegiate church, a superb example of the Perpendicular style, is unusual in that it has transepts but no central tower, though it does have an imposing west tower. The spacious interior is of almost cathedral-like proportions.

🖉 The walk starts in the Market Place. Turn right along the road towards the church and castle but almost immediately turn left, at a public footpath sign, along an enclosed tarmac path. After crossing a footbridge over the disused Horncastle Canal, turn left alongside it and cross a footbridge over the River Bain to a T-junction Ⓐ.

Turn right beside the river and, at a waymarked post, follow the path to the left, passing to the left of a pool. Continue along what is now a track, climb a stile beside a gate and keep ahead to a road Ⓑ. Turn right for about ¹/₄ mile (400m) if you wish to visit the Battle of Britain Memorial Flight, where there are World War II aircraft and a visitor centre with displays and exhibits of the battle.

The route continues to the left into Coningsby. At a road junction, bear slightly left along Silver Street, then turn right into Park Lane and follow the road around a left-hand bend to a T-junction Ⓒ. Turn right, turn left along Wharfe Lane (signposted to Tattershall Thorpe and Woodhall Spa) and immediately after crossing a bridge over the River Bain, turn left to climb a stile Ⓓ. Now follows a delightful part of the route as you continue across riverside meadows and over several stiles, with fine views ahead of the tower of Coningsby's medieval church, noted for the huge clock on the west tower.

Cross a tarmac path to the right of a footbridge, climb the stile opposite, continue by the river and go through a kissing-gate onto a road. Turn left over a bridge, turn right through a kissing-gate and continue along the other bank of the Bain to a footbridge Ⓐ. Here you rejoin the outward route and turn right over the bridge to retrace your steps to the starting point. ●

Thornton Abbey

Start	Thornton Abbey
Distance	3½ miles (5.6km)
Approximate time	1½ hours
Parking	Thornton Abbey, by the picnic site
Refreshments	None
Ordnance Survey maps	Explorer 284 (Grimsby, Cleethorpes & Immingham), Landranger 113 (Grimsby, Louth & Market Rasen)

The walk is almost a perfect square, and its chief focal point, the imposing gatehouse of Thornton Abbey, is in sight for most of the way amidst the flat terrain. The views are particularly impressive on the last stretch between Thornton Abbey station and the start. Although this is a quiet walk with a genuinely remote feel, glimpses of the oil refineries of Humberside on the horizon are a reminder that the 21st century is not far away.

Thornton Abbey was founded as an Augustinian priory in 1139, raised to abbey status in 1148 and suppressed by Henry VIII in 1539. Little survives of the church and monastic buildings, except for part of the chapter-house, but the brick and stone gatehouse is one of the largest and most elaborate in the country. Built in the late 14th century, it was partly fortified, and the approach is lined with redbrick arcaded walling.

Facing the abbey gatehouse, turn left to the road and bear right along it. At a public footpath sign, turn right through a kissing-gate, keep ahead to cross a footbridge over a drain, climb

Ruins of Thornton Abbey

steps and continue along the right-hand edge of a field. After going through a kissing-gate, the easiest route would be to continue straight ahead but the line of the right of way is to bear right to keep by a line of trees on the right and follow the curve of the field edge to the left to go through another kissing-gate.

Turn right to cross a footbridge and bear slightly left across the field to cross another footbridge over East Halton Beck. Continue along the left-hand field edge, curving right, and turn left through a waymarked gate and up through bushes to a road. Turn right and at a public footpath sign **Ⓐ**, turn right along a track. The track keeps along the left-hand edge of fields and, in the corner of the last field, follow the track first to the right and then turn left through a gate. Walk along an enclosed track, which later continues across a field, rising gently to go through a gate onto a lane **Ⓑ**.

Turn right along the winding lane to a T-junction, turn left (in the Ulceby direction) and, just after a right-hand bend, go over a level-crossing and immediately turn right along a track **Ⓒ**. The track curves left to enter a field and, at a waymarked post, turn right along its right-hand edge. Keep in a straight line along the right-hand edge of a series of fields, parallel to the rail line and with a drain below on the right. Where the drain ends, follow the field edge as it bends first right and then left and continue to a road by Thornton Abbey station.

Do not turn left to the road but turn right through a gate **Ⓓ**, recross the railway line at the end of the station platform and go through another gate. With a magnificent view of the abbey gatehouse ahead, follow a grassy track back to the start. ●

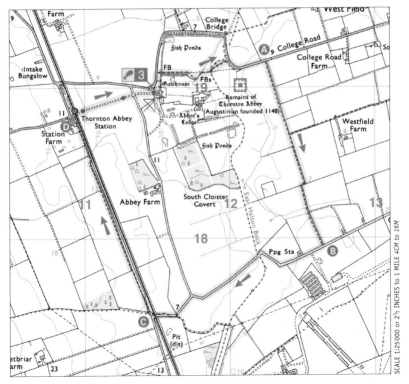

SCALE 1:25 000 or 2½ INCHES to 1 MILE 4CM to 1KM

Spalding

Start	Spalding, Ayscoughfee Hall Gardens
Distance	4½ miles (7.2km)
Approximate time	2 hours
Parking	Spalding
Refreshments	Pubs and cafés at Spalding
Ordnance Survey maps	Explorer 249 (Spalding & Holbeach), Landranger 131 (Boston & Spalding)

This easy and relaxing route is entirely along the banks of the waterways that surround the centre of Spalding – the River Welland and the Coronation Channel. The latter was dug as part of the town's flood defences following the devastating floods of 1947 and was opened in 1953. Spalding is the centre of Britain's bulb industry so in spring the town looks at its most colourful with its superb displays of daffodils and tulips.

The placid tree-lined river, its banks lined by handsome brick houses, gives a distinctly Dutch air to Spalding. This is reinforced in springtime when the town is a riot of tulips and other spring flowers, especially during the Flower Parade held in May. One of the most colourful parts

Springtime in Spalding

of the town is Ayscoughfee Hall Gardens where the walk begins. Ayscoughfee Hall, built in the late medieval period by a wealthy wool merchant, now houses a museum and tourist information centre. From the hall, the view across the gardens and bowling-green is dominated by the tower and spire of Spalding's large, imposing and unusually wide medieval church, one of the glories of Lincolnshire.

🖉 Start by the hall, bowling-green and café and, with your back to the hall, turn left and left again to exit the gardens and walk along a tree-lined tarmac drive to a road. Turn right, turn left to cross a footbridge over the River Welland and turn left alongside the river. At the second bridge, turn left to recross it, turn right along the other bank and, just after passing Churchill Drive, turn left onto an enclosed path beside the Coronation Channel Ⓐ. After crossing a road, the path follows the curve of the channel to the left. At the

next lane, turn right to cross a bridge over the channel.

Turn left **B** onto a pleasant path along the east side of the channel – to the right there are views across bulb fields – as far as the fourth bridge (second road bridge) **C**. If here in the spring, it would be worthwhile making a short detour at this point and keeping ahead to visit Springfields Gardens, in order to see the magnificent display of tulips and other spring flowers. Otherwise, turn left over the bridge towards a redbrick Victorian church,

turn right along a track beside the channel and, where it bears left, keep ahead along the top of a grassy embankment.

After crossing a road, pass beside a gate, continue to where the Coronation Channel meets the Welland and turn sharp left **D** alongside the river. The grassy path emerges onto a road. Turn right over the second bridge and turn left **E** onto an attractive tarmac path – part footpath, part cycleway – along the west side of the river. Descend steps to pass under a footbridge and, after crossing a road, turn left to recross the river via a footbridge. Turn right and retrace your steps to the start. ●

North Carlton and Scampton

Start	Till Bridge Lane Viewpoint, at corner of A1500 and B1398
Distance	4½ miles (7.2km)
Approximate time	2 hours
Parking	Till Bridge Lane Viewpoint
Refreshments	Pub at Scampton
Ordnance Survey maps	Explorer 272 (Lincoln), Landranger 121 (Lincoln & Newark-on-Trent)

From the starting point on Lincoln Edge, the views westwards across the flat expanses of the Trent valley are both extensive and superb. After a gentle descent from the edge, the route passes through the quiet villages of North Carlton and Scampton, both of which have interesting churches, before returning to the ridge-top.

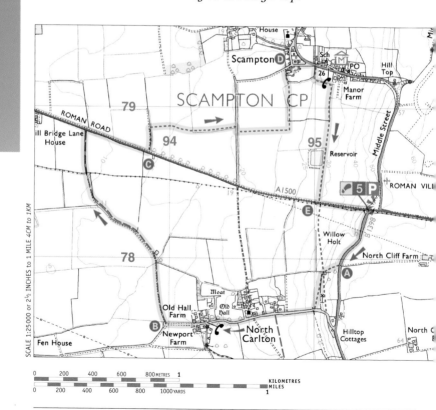

SCALE 1:25 000 or 2½ INCHES to 1 MILE 4CM to 1KM

| 0 | 200 | 400 | 600 | 800 METRES | 1 |
| 0 | 200 | 400 | 600 | 800 | 1000 YARDS |

KILOMETRES
MILES

Scampton church

Start by walking along the B1398 (signposted to Burton and Lincoln) and, after ¼ mile (400m), turn right Ⓐ at a public footpath sign and head downhill across a field, veering left and making for a hedge corner. Turn left and continue across the field, keeping roughly in line with telegraph poles and, on the far side, go through a hedge gap onto a lane.

Turn right and follow the lane through the hamlet of North Carlton, passing to the left of the church. This is a mainly Georgian building, rare for a small village church, with a 15th-century tower. Where the lane curves left, turn right Ⓑ, at a public bridleway sign, along a tarmac track and, after bearing left to pass in front of barns, continue along a track to where it curves left. At this point, keep ahead along the right-hand edge of two fields to a road, turn right and, at a public footpath sign, turn left along the right-hand edge of a field Ⓒ.

Look out for where a yellow waymark directs you to turn right through a hedge gap, cross a plank footbridge and keep straight ahead across a field, making for a hedge gap on the far side. Go through, keep ahead across the next field and go through a hedge gap onto a lane. Cross over, continue along a track across a field and, at a T-junction, turn left and walk along the right-hand edge of a field to reach a lane on the edge of Scampton Ⓓ.

Keep ahead to visit the mainly 15th-century church; otherwise the route continues to the right through the village. Turn right at a T-junction and, at a public footpath sign, turn right through a fence gap and walk along the right-hand edge of a field. Turn left in the field corner and, in front of a barn, turn right along a track. The track passes between reservoir embankments. Look out for a yellow-waymarked post where you turn right over a ditch. Turn left, continue along a broad grassy track to a road Ⓔ and turn left uphill to return to the start. ●

Barton and the River Humber

Start	Barton Waterside, Clay Pits car park
Distance	5½ miles (8.9km)
Approximate time	2½ hours
Parking	Barton Waterside
Refreshments	Pubs and cafés at Barton-Upon-Humber
Ordnance Survey maps	Explorer 281 (Ancholme Valley), Landranger 112 (Scunthorpe)

The wide-ranging views on this walk include the northern slopes of the Lincolnshire Wolds, up and down the Humber estuary and across the river to the southern edge of the Yorkshire Wolds, plus, of course, stunning views of the Humber Bridge near where the walk begins. The route takes you through the small town of Barton-Upon-Humber, passing its celebrated Saxon church, before heading across fields for a final 1¹⁄₂ mile (2.4km) stretch beside the estuary.

Barton Clay Pits and the adjoining Far Ings Nature Reserve comprise a series of flooded clay pits along the south bank of the Humber estuary, dug for the making of tiles and bricks. They are now a haven for wildlife. The starting point is an excellent place from which to appreciate the beauty and elegance of the Humber Bridge, opened in 1981 and one of the suspension bridges with the longest spans in the world. The length of the main span is 4,626ft (1,410m).

✏ Start by facing the river, turn left and, at the far end of the car park,

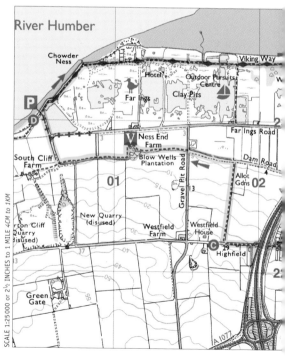

take a path through trees. Turn left at a T-junction in front of a pool, walk along a straight path to a road, turn left and, at a T-junction Ⓐ, turn right into Barton-Upon-Humber. Pass the station to reach a junction of roads and continue along the narrow street ahead (Fleetgate), passing to the right of the White Swan. Take the second street on the left (High Street), bear left at a junction to continue along High Street and then Burgate, walk past St Mary's Church and, at a T-junction, take the tarmac path opposite to the Saxon church of St Peter Ⓑ.

The close proximity of two outstanding medieval churches is an indication that Barton was a prosperous town and important Humber port, until eclipsed from the late 13th century onwards by the rise of Hull on the opposite side of the river. St Mary's, which dates from the 12th century – with later additions – is a large and impressive town church but major interest is inevitably centred on St Peter's for its Saxon architecture. The west end and tower remain of the original 10th-century church,; the rest was rebuilt and added to over the following centuries.

Retrace your steps along Burgate and High Street and, at the junction, do not follow your earlier route by continuing to the right along High Street but bear slightly left, along Hungate to a crossroads. Turn right and, where the main road bends right, keep ahead along Westfield Road. At the end of the road, keep ahead along a tarmac track to pass under the A15, climb steps and continue along a narrow lane. At a public footpath sign, turn right Ⓒ on to a path that heads gently downhill along the left-hand edge of a field. Ahead are magnificent views of the Humber Bridge and the estuary, with the southern slopes of the Yorkshire Wolds on the horizon.

Continue along the right-hand edge of the next field, in the corner turn left and turn right to cross a footbridge over a drain on to a narrow lane. Turn left to a T-junction, keep ahead across a meadow, by the drain on the left, cross a footbridge and, at a public footpath sign to South Ferriby, continue across the meadow, later keeping by its left-hand edge. Go through a hedge gap in the corner and immediately turn right, at a byway sign, along a hedge-lined track to reach a T-junction in front of the river Ⓓ.

Turn right, go through a kissing-gate and walk along the top of an embankment between the Humber estuary on the left and the pools of the Far Ings Nature Reserve on the right. About $1/4$ mile (400m) after passing under the Humber Bridge, turn right down steps to return to the start. ●

Tennyson Country

Start	Tetford
Distance	5 miles (8km)
Approximate time	2½ hours
Parking	Roadside parking at Tetford by the church
Refreshments	Pub at Tetford
Ordnance Survey maps	Explorer 273 (Lincolnshire Wolds South), Landranger 122 (Skegness & Horncastle)

The first part of this route in the heart of 'Tennyson Country' is along the line of a Roman road to the east of the village of Tetford. It continues over the wolds, dropping into the tiny hamlet of Somersby, where Tennyson was born and brought up. From here, lanes, tracks and field paths lead back to the start. There are fine views over the wolds from the higher points on the walk.

Start by the mainly 15th-century greenstone church, walk along the narrow lane to the left of it and, at a public footpath sign, turn right through a gate. Walk through the churchyard to a stile, climb it, and the route now continues in a straight line across a field, following the line of a Roman road that ran from Lincoln to Burgh le Marsh. It first passes through several lines of trees (old field boundaries), keeps along the left-hand edge of a line of trees, then goes through a wide gap in that line and finally heads across to a waymarked stile on the far side.

Climb the stile and bear slightly right across the next field to cross a foot-bridge. Walk along the right-hand edge of a field, cross a footbridge, keep along the left-hand edge of the next field, cross a footbridge in the corner and go through a kissing-gate. Head across a field corner to go through another kissing-gate, cross another footbridge, continue across the next field, cross a

footbridge and keep ahead to a footpath post. Cross a track, continue across a field, cross a footbridge on the far side, turn right **A** along the right-hand edge of a field and cross one more footbridge onto a lane.

Turn left and, at a public bridleway sign, turn right **B** along an enclosed uphill path, which passes along the right-hand edge of Willow Bank Wood at the top. From here there are superb views over the wolds. The path descends

Descending to Somersby

but, after about 200 yds (183m), turn right **C** through a wide gap in the hedge and continue across fields to a T-junction. Turn left along a track down into a dip and up again to another T-junction, turn right, and the track bends left to Wardenhill Farm. Follow the track to the right in front of the farm buildings and the track later curves left and heads downhill – a grand view ahead over the wolds here – to Somersby House Farm.

In front of the farm, turn left along a lane to a T-junction **D** and turn right, passing to the left of Somersby church. Alfred, Lord Tennyson was born in this quiet and remote hamlet in 1809, the son of the rector, and lived here for most of his early life. His birthplace is a private residence and not open to the public. The small, plain greenstone church has a display about the poet and his life in this part of Lincolnshire.

Continue along the lane, following it around right- and left-hand bends. After almost 1 mile (1.6km), turn right **E** at a public bridleway sign, along a track by the left-hand edge of a field. The track narrows to a path that bears slightly left and becomes enclosed. At a footpath post, turn right along the left-hand edge of a field, in the corner continue along an enclosed, tree-lined path and climb a stile onto a road. Turn left and take the first road on the right (East Road), which leads back to the starting point.

Claythorpe Mill and the Swaby valley

Start	Aby, village hall
Distance	5½ miles (8.9km)
Approximate time	2½ hours
Parking	Roadside parking at Aby near the village hall
Refreshments	Pub at South Thoresby, café at Claythorpe Mill
Ordnance Survey maps	Explorer 274 (Skegness, Alford & Spilsby), Landranger 122 (Skegness & Horncastle)

This walk on the eastern fringes of the wolds links four quiet hamlets and passes a picturesque watermill. From Aby you head across fields to Claythorpe Mill and then on through the wide valley of the Great Eau to Belleau. The route continues to the edge of Swaby, and this is followed by a delightful ramble through the beautiful and steep-sided Swaby valley and on to South Thoresby. A combination of field paths, lanes and tracks leads back to the start.

The walk starts in front of the village hall at Aby at the junction of School Lane and New Street. With your back to the hall, turn right to the end of School Lane and turn left, at a public footpath sign Ⓐ, along a tarmac track to Paddock House. Go through two gates in quick succession, walk across a field to climb a stile on the far side and keep along the right-hand edge of the next field.

At a hedge corner, bear slightly right and continue across the field to the far corner. Turn right along a lane, passing under a disused railway bridge, and take the first lane on the left Ⓑ to Claythorpe Mill. This attractive 18th-century watermill, situated on the River Great Eau, is now the focal point of a wildfowl garden and is open daily from March to October.

Continue past the mill, and the lane curves right to a T-junction. Turn left

and, where the lane curves right, turn left Ⓒ at a public footpath sign, along a track and turn right over a stile. Turn left along the left-hand edge of a field, follow it to the right, keeping beside a stream, and bear left to cross a footbridge over the stream. Continue in a straight line across the next field, making for a public footpath sign, where you emerge onto a lane, and turn left into Belleau.

Head gently uphill, bending right to pass the Victorian church, and continue to a T-junction. Turn right and, at a public footpath sign, turn left Ⓓ along the left-hand edge of a field, by woodland on the left. At the corner of the wood, keep straight ahead across the field, passing to the right of a small clump of trees, and continue to a hedge gap on the far side. Go through, keep ahead across the next field – the houses of Swaby are seen below – and on the far side, continue along the right-hand edge of woodland. Look out for where you climb a waymarked stile, head downhill along a tree-lined path and climb another stile onto a tarmac track on the edge of Swaby **E**. Turn left and, where the track ends, bear left at a public bridleway sign to South Thoresby, along a grassy track above a pool to a stile. After climbing it, the route continues beside Swaby Beck through the lovely Swaby valley. Go through a gate, keep ahead through the valley, ignore a permissive footpath sign on the right but, at the next footpath post, bear right through scrub and trees and to

enter a field.

Walk along the right-hand edge of the field and look out for a yellow-waymarked post that directs you to turn right through another area of trees and scrub. Cross a footbridge, keep ahead along boardwalks to a public footpath sign and turn left. Head across a field, veering right away from its left-hand edge, walk along more boardwalks and continue to a footbridge over the Great Eau on the far side. Cross it and keep ahead along the right-hand edge of the next field to a stile in the corner **F**.

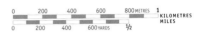

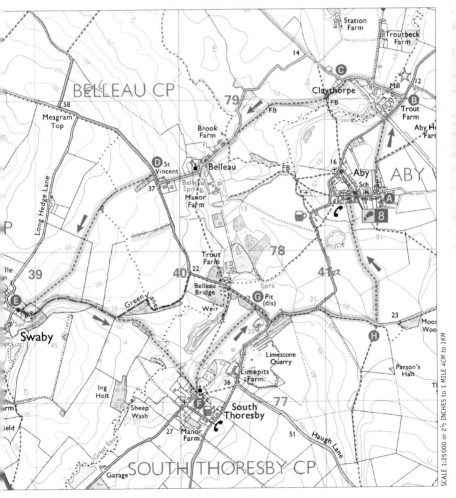

Do not climb the stile if continuing along the route but do so if you wish to visit the church and pub at South Thoresby. The church is immediately to the left, a small brick Georgian building dating from the 1730s. For the pub, keep along a tarmac track, which curves right to a road, and turn left.

To continue with the route, turn sharp left in front of the stile, initially along the right-hand edge of the field but, where the edge bears right, keep ahead and in front you see two way-marked stiles. Make for the right-hand one of these, climb it and walk across a field. On the far side, continue along a grassy track to a lane **G**, turn right to a T-junction and turn left. Turn right along a lane signposted to Greenfield and Alford and, at a public footpath sign, turn left **H** and head across a field, making for a waymarked post just to the left of a tree.

Keep in the same direction across the next field, heading towards a public footpath sign at a hedge corner, and continue beside the hedge to the corner of the field. Turn right through a gap, walk along the left-hand edge of the next field and turn left to cross a foot-bridge over a ditch. Keep ahead across a field, continue along an enclosed track to a lane and turn right to return to the start.   ●

In the Swaby valley

Stamford, Easton on the Hill and Tinwell

Start	Stamford, Red Lion Square
Distance	5½ miles (8.9km)
Approximate time	2½ hours
Parking	Stamford
Refreshments	Pubs and cafés at Stamford, pub at Easton on the Hill, pub at Tinwell
Ordnance Survey maps	Explorer 234 (Rutland Water & Stamford), Landranger 141 (Kettering & Corby)

This is a most attractive walk, the first and last parts of which are across delightful riverside meadows beside the Welland. In between you pass through two beautiful villages, and there are fine views over the valley, especially looking across to Stamford. As the town is at the far south-western tip of Lincolnshire and close to three county boundaries, there is some 'border hopping' and, although a relatively short route, it briefly enters both Northamptonshire and Rutland. Leave plenty of time to explore Stamford, one of England's most attractive and historic towns.

A 17th-century traveller described Stamford 'as fine a built town all of stone as may be seen' and this is still true today as the town is undeniably attractive and remains remarkably unspoilt. Most of its handsome stone buildings date from the 17th and 18th centuries, and it has an outstanding collection of medieval churches, whose towers and spires make a particularly fine sight when viewed from the riverside meadows on the last part of the walk. There is no single outstanding building, it is the whole harmonious package which makes a walk around Stamford so rewarding.

The walk starts in Red Lion Square. In one corner of it, at a footpath sign to The Meadows, walk along the alley called Horseshoe Lane into Sheep Market. Keep ahead along Castle Dyke and cross a road into the riverside meadow. Cross a bridge over an arm of the river, bear right and head diagonally across the meadow to a gate in the far corner Ⓐ. Go through, take the way-marked path ahead across the meadows and cross a metal footbridge (Broadeng Bridge) over the Welland, here entering Northamptonshire.

Turn right beside the river and at a fork Ⓑ – there are Jurassic Way and Macmillan Way signs here – take the left-hand path and go under a bridge under the A1. Cross a plank footbridge, keep ahead across a field and, on the far side, climb steps, cross another footbridge and carefully cross a railway line. Descend steps on the other side, continue along an enclosed path and,

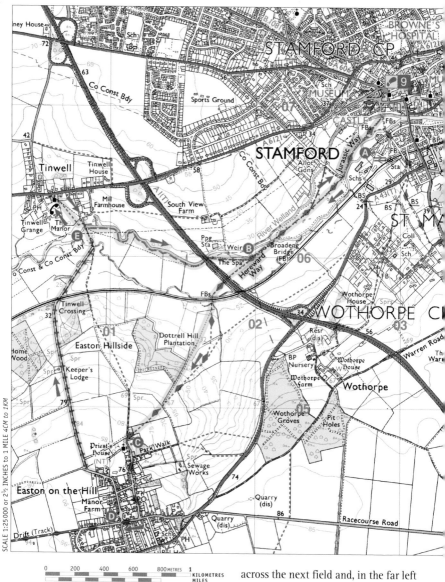

SCALE 1:25000 or 2½ INCHES to 1 MILE 4CM to 1KM

on emerging into a field, keep ahead across it and go through a gate in the far corner.

Walk along a gently ascending, tree-lined track that continues along the right-hand edge of a field and, where the track curves left, turn right through a hedge gap. Continue across a field, climb a stile and bear right across the next field to another stile. After climbing it, keep in the same direction

across the next field and, in the far left corner, go through a fence gap and turn left **C** along Church Street into Easton on the Hill, passing to the left of the imposing medieval church. This is a beautiful village of attractive old cottages and handsome houses, all built – like those at Stamford – from the local limestone.

At a T-junction by the war memorial in the village centre, turn right along High Street and take the first road on the right **D** (West Street), passing the Priest's House, which is a rare example of a medieval priest's dwelling, now owned by the National Trust. Where the road ends, keep ahead along a broad, enclosed track which heads steadily downhill. Gaps in the trees on the right reveal fine views across the fields to the skyline of Stamford.

At the bottom of the hill, recross the railway line and continue along an enclosed path, which bends left to a bridge over the River Welland Ⓔ. By now the route has entered Rutland.

The walk continues to the right before crossing the bridge but for a brief detour into Tinwell, cross the bridge and immediately, at a footpath post, turn left over a waymarked stile. Head diagonally across grass – crossing a

drive – climb a stile in the corner and turn right along an enclosed path. Climb a stile, follow a path across a meadow towards the church and climb another stile in the far corner. Walk along a tarmac path through the churchyard, passing to the right of the medieval church, noted for its saddle-back tower, to the main street.

Retrace your steps to the bridge over the Welland Ⓔ, cross it and, at a public bridleway sign, turn left and keep by its meandering bank. Shortly after passing under a bridge under the A1, you rejoin the outward route Ⓑ and retrace your steps to the start, enjoying the superb views ahead of the towers and spires of Stamford from the riverside meadows.●

Riverside meadows at Stamford

Boston and the River Witham

Start	Boston, Market Place
Distance	6½ miles (10.5km)
Approximate time	3 hours
Parking	Boston
Refreshments	Pubs and cafés at Boston, pub at Cowbridge, tearoom at Maud Foster Windmill
Ordnance Survey maps	Explorer 261 (Boston), Landranger 131 (Boston & Spalding)

Almost the whole of this triangular-shaped walk to the north of Boston is beside water: Maud Foster Drain, Frith Bank Drain and the River Witham. The last 2½ miles (4km) along the banks of the river are particularly attractive and memorable, especially for the impressive views of Boston Stump, the tallest church tower in the country. Leave plenty of time to explore the interesting and historic port of Boston.

Between the 12th and the 15th centuries, Boston was one of the greatest ports in England, with a flourishing trade across the North Sea and Baltic. A slump in the wool trade and the silting up of the Witham caused it to decline in the 16th century but the agricultural development of the drained Fens and subsequent dredging of the river led to its revival in the 18th and 19th centuries, and it still functions as a port. The most striking and obvious reflection of its medieval prosperity is St Botolph's Church, built in the 14th century and one of the finest and largest parish churches in the country. The spacious and lofty interior has a cathedral-like appearance but its most outstanding feature is the 15th-century tower, 272ft (83m) high and the tallest in England, always referred to as 'Boston Stump'. It is a landmark for miles around, dominating the flat landscape of the Fens and visible from many points on the Lincolnshire Wolds, around 20 miles (32km) away.

Start in the Market Place by the church and walk along Strait Bargate, which broadens out into Wide Bargate. Keep along its left side and, where the road divides, take the right-hand road and cross a bridge over Maud Foster Drain. Turn left along Willoughby Road Ⓐ, passing Maud Foster Windmill, built in 1819 and the tallest working windmill in the country. Unusually it has five sails.

Continue along the road beside the drain and, just after a level-crossing, you reach a T-junction to the right of a bridge. Keep ahead through a gate, walk

0	200	400	600	800 METRES	**1**	
						KILOMETRES
						MILES
0	200	400	600 YARDS	½		

along a track and, where it ends in front of a house, turn right and follow the edge of a garden round to the left to a T-junction. Turn left – there is a junction of five drains here at Cowbridge – cross a footbridge over the Maud Foster Drain to a road and turn right. After crossing a bridge over Frith Bank Drain, turn left **B** along a road beside it. Across the fields to the left are distant views of Boston Stump.

After just over $1\frac{1}{2}$ miles (2.4km), turn left **C** at a public footpath sign to cross a footbridge over the drain, turn left along a grassy bank beside it and, at the next public footpath sign, turn sharp right along an enclosed path. Follow the path around first a left bend and then a right bend and go through a gate onto a riverside path **D**. Turn left and follow this attractive path beside the Witham back to Boston. Ahead there are superb views of Boston Stump almost all the time.

After passing under a railway bridge and beside Grand Sluice Lock, turn right over a bridge **E** and turn left along a tarmac path on the other bank of the river, which emerges onto a road. Keep ahead, turn left **F** to recross the River Witham via a footbridge and continue along Church Lane into the Market Place.

Boston Stump and the River Witham

Isle of Axholme

Start	Epworth, Church Walk car park
Distance	6½ miles (10.5km)
Approximate time	3 hours
Parking	Epworth
Refreshments	Pubs and cafés at Epworth
Ordnance Survey maps	Explorer 280 (Isle of Axholme), Landranger 112 (Scunthorpe)

The Isle of Axholme is an 'island' of slightly higher ground that rises above the flat landscape of the Trent flood plain in north Lincolnshire, near the South Yorkshire and Nottinghamshire borders. This is very much 'Wesley Country' as both John Wesley and his brother Charles were born at Epworth. The walk starts by the church where their father was rector, passes the house in which the family lived and goes on to explore the pleasant countryside around Epworth, which offers wide and extensive views.

The small town of Epworth is known the world over as the birthplace of John Wesley, the founder of Methodism. His father, Samuel Wesley, was rector here from 1695 to 1735, and John was born in 1703. The attractive medieval church, in which both John and his hymn-writing brother Charles were baptised, dates mainly from the 13th century, apart from the Perpendicular tower. In later years, John was denied access because of his religious beliefs and had to deliver his powerful sermons outside, either from his father's grave or from the Market Cross. The Wesley Memorial Methodist Church in High Street was erected in 1889 in honour of John and Charles.

From the car park, take the road that leads into the Market Place and turn left along Albion Hill. At a T-junction, turn left along Rectory Street, passing to the right of the Old Rectory. This handsome Georgian house is a later rebuilding of the one which was the Wesley family home for 40 years. It contains a large selection of Wesley memorabilia.

At a public footpath sign just beyond the Old Rectory, turn right along a track **A**. Pass beside a gate, keep ahead, passing to the left of a disused wind-mill, and turn right along a track that curves right to a road **B**. Cross over

The Old Rectory at Epworth

and take the hedge-lined track opposite, which continues first along the right-hand edge of fields and then heads across fields towards woodland. At a T-junction, turn left along a path, follow it around a right bend, turn left at the next T-junction and then turn right to continue along the left-hand edge of a field.

Keep ahead to pass under a disused railway bridge, continue across a field and cross a footbridge over a drain. Walk across the next field, bearing slightly left and making for a hedge gap, where you climb an embankment and pass through another hedge gap. Continue more or less in a straight line, first along an enclosed path, by a line of trees on the right, then by the right-hand edge of a field and finally along a track, to emerge onto a lane **C**.

Turn sharp right alongside the woodlands of Epworth Turbary Nature Reserve on the left and, at the corner of the wood, turn left along a track, which keeps by the right-hand edge of the trees.

The track bends left to continue alongside the wood and after $\frac{1}{4}$ mile (400m) bends right towards a farm. After passing to the right of the farm,

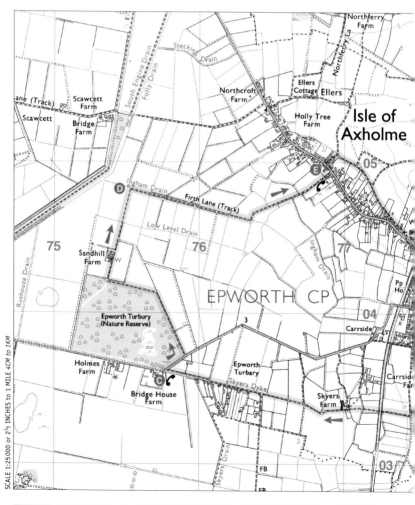

Epworth church

climb a stile and keep ahead along the right-hand edge of fields to a T-junction by a waymarked post **D**. Turn right along a straight track, by a drain on the left, then at the next waymarked post turn left to cross a bridge over the drain. The track turns

right to head across fields, becomes enclosed and continues to a road **E**.

Turn left and at a public footpath sign, turn right along a track to a T-junction. Turn right to continue along a track by the bottom edge of fields and, where it peters out, keep ahead across grass to a waymarked post and turn right to the road. Turn left and, at a public footpath sign, turn left along a paved path **F**, which becomes enclosed and heads gently uphill towards a disused windmill. Where the path bends left, turn right over a stile, walk along the left-hand edge of a field and, in the corner, turn left over a stile. Turn right beside a gate and continue along the right-hand edge of a field towards a converted windmill. Although at a height of only 66ft (20m), the views to the right over Epworth are outstanding.

On emerging on to a road to the left of the converted windmill, turn right and, at a public footpath sign, turn left along the left-hand edge of a field. The track continues across fields and bends right to head towards Epworth. At a road, turn right **G** along a track towards the church and, where the track starts to descend, turn left through a hedge gap and head across a recreation and picnic area to the start. ●

Sea banks of the Wash

Start	Moulton Marsh Nature Reserve, take first lane on the left (Middle Marsh Road) to the south of Fosdyke Bridge and turn left at a T-junction
Distance	6½ miles (10.5km)
Approximate time	3 hours
Parking	Moulton Marsh Nature Reserve
Refreshments	None
Ordnance Survey maps	Explorer 249 (Spalding & Holbeach), Landranger 131 (Boston & Spalding)

Even though much of the marshland is cultivated, the traffic on the busy A17 can be heard at times and Boston Stump stands out clearly on the horizon to the north, there is nothing to equal the sense of remoteness and isolation experienced by walking across the bleak, extensive and formerly treacherous marshes of the Wash. The whole of this route is along various embankments which were built to contain the sea and are evidence of the ever-changing coastline in this area. The final stretch is beside the River Welland. Inevitably the immense views extend for miles across a mixture of farmland, saltmarsh, tidal flats and water.

Start by turning right out of the car park along a lane, follow it around a left-hand bend and, just after crossing a drain, turn left through a gate, at a public bridleway sign **A**. The remainder of the walk – at least up to point **E** – is along the top of old sea banks, constructed at various times to hold back the waters of the North Sea.

Walk along the top of the embankment, at a footpath post follow it to the right **B** and, after almost 2 miles (3.2km), turn left, at a public bridleway sign **C**, along a narrower embankment to a T-junction **D**. A brief detour to the right will enable you to look across the marshes to the sea but the route

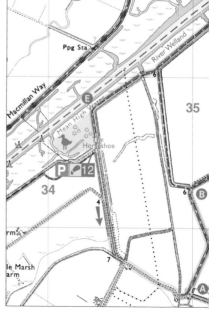

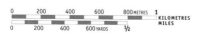

continues to the left. Over to the right the distinctive landmark of Boston Stump is visible on the skyline, and to the left you look across the broad expanses of Moulton Marsh.

The embankment later keeps above the River Welland on the right and, just after passing beside a gate, you leave it by turning left along a track **E**. Pass beside another gate and turn right, back into the nature reserve car park. ●

Marshes near the Wash

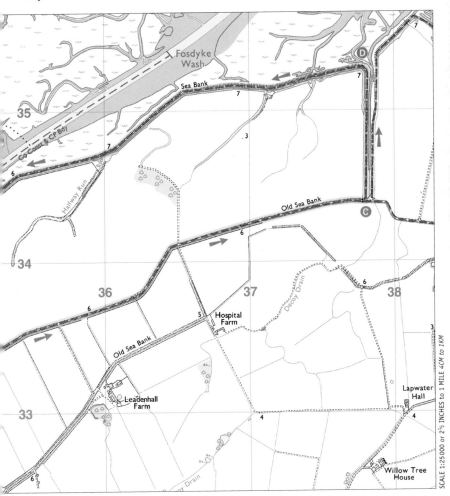

Vale of Belvoir

Start	Woolsthorpe By Belvoir
Distance	6½ miles (10.5km)
Approximate time	3 hours
Parking	Roadside parking at Woolsthorpe
Refreshments	Pub at Woolsthorpe, pub at Woolsthorpe Bridge
Ordnance Survey maps	Explorer 247 (Grantham), Landranger 130 Grantham)

From many points on this walk on the Lincolnshire-Leicestershire border, there are fine views across the broad expanses of the Vale of Belvoir. The striking profile of Belvoir Castle is in sight for much of the way, seen from many different angles as the route describes a wide arc to the north of the castle. Almost half the walk is along the towpath of the delightful and peaceful Grantham Canal.

Woolsthorpe By Belvoir is an attractive village of ironstone cottages, presided over by a fine Victorian church.

Start by the post office and small village green, turn southwards towards the church and almost immediately turn right along Belvoir Lane. Where the lane ends, keep ahead along a path and at a public footpath sign, turn right to cross a footbridge over the River Devon.

Climb a stile, keep ahead by a line of trees on the right, climb another stile and continue along the right-hand edge of a field. On this part of the walk you enjoy what are probably the finest views of Belvoir Castle, ancestral home of the earls and later dukes of Rutland. Although its towers and walls give it a medieval appearance, these were for effect only as the castle was predominantly rebuilt in the early 19th century when it was fashionable to build in a 'romantic' medieval style.

In the field corner, follow a Jubilee Way sign to the right, walk along the left-hand edge of a field and climb a

stile on to a road **A**. Turn left, follow the road around a right-hand bend and, at the castle entrance and car park, turn right along the road signposted to Redmile and Bottesford. After ¹/₂ mile (800m), turn right **B** along a narrow lane and, after the second farm, the way continues along a rough track. Immediately after crossing a bridge over the Grantham Canal, turn right **C** onto the towpath and keep along it for the next 2¹/₂ miles (4km).

The canal was constructed between 1793 and 1797 to link Grantham with the River Trent at Nottingham. On this section it goes round a long right-hand curve, and there are extensive views across the vale and constantly changing views of the castle. After passing a lock, leave the canal by climbing a stile and turning right **D** over Woolsthorpe Bridge (no. 61). Walk past the Rutland Arms and along a tarmac track to a road **E** and turn left to return to Woolsthorpe.

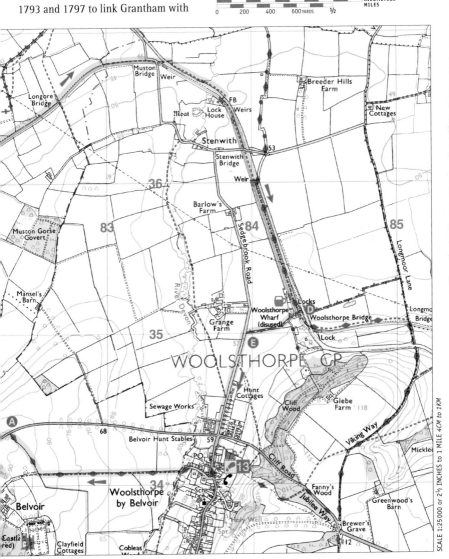

Donington and the Bain valley

Donington and the Bain valley

Start	Donington on Bain
Distance	6 miles (9.7km)
Approximate time	3 hours
Parking	Roadside parking at Donington on Bain
Refreshments	Pub at Donington on Bain
Ordnance Survey maps	Explorer 282 (Lincolnshire Wolds North), Landranger 122 (Skegness & Horncastle)

This fine walk begins with an easy climb onto a broad ridge and continues along the ridge, from which there are superb views over the Bain valley. It proceeds into the hamlet of Gayton le Wold and climbs again before descending into the valley, passing through the site of a deserted medieval village. The final stretch is a beautiful and relaxing stroll beside the River Bain, passing a picturesque mill just before the end.

Donington on Bain is a most attractive village with a fine location on the River Bain sheltering below the wolds. The medieval church has a sturdy-looking Norman tower.

The walk begins by the church and post office. Walk along Main Road, passing to the right of the church. Where the road bears right on the edge of the village, turn left Ⓐ over a stile, at a public footpath sign, and walk along an enclosed track. Head gently uphill, passing through woodlands. Then, on reaching a track at a public bridleway sign, turn left along it Ⓑ. As the track continues along the left-hand edge of a field, there are grand views to the left over the Bain valley, and Lincoln Cathedral can be seen on the horizon.

Cross a lane, keep along the left-hand edge of fields and, where the track bends right to continue along the left-hand field edge, turn left through a hedge gap and walk along a straight track, later bearing right along the left-hand edge of a field to a T-junction. Turn left on to a track that heads gently downhill to a lane Ⓒ and turn right along the narrow lane, which descends into the hamlet of Gayton le Wold, passing the small, brick Victorian church.

At a public footpath sign, turn left Ⓓ over a stile and bear left across a field to cross a footbridge. Continue in the same direction across the next field, making for the far corner, where you climb a double stile and turn right along a track. There is a quarry to the left. Climb a stile, turn left Ⓔ gently downhill along a lane – the mast of Belmont Transmitting Station is directly ahead – and look out for public

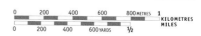

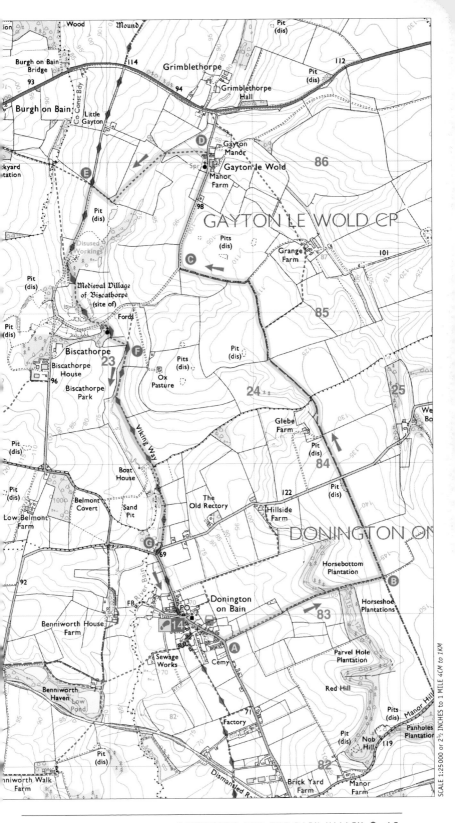

SCALE 1:25000 or 2½ INCHES to 1 MILE 4CM to 1KM

footpath and Viking Way signs, which direct you to bear left along a grassy path through trees to a stile. After climbing it, head downhill across a field to a footbridge over the River Bain. Bumps in the field indicate that this is the site of the deserted medieval village of Biscarthorpe.

After crossing the footbridge, bear left across grass, cross a lane to a public footpath sign in front of a house and bear right along the right-hand edge of a meadow, passing to the left of Biscarthorpe's fine Victorian church. This was built in 1853 by the owner of nearby Biscarthorpe House after the original church fell into decay. Climb a stile, turn left along a fence-lined path, recross the Bain via a footbridge and turn right onto a path beside it **F**. The route now continues across fields by the river, over stiles and footbridges – at one point the river broadens out into an attractive lake – finally climbing a stile on to a lane **G**.

Turn right to a T-junction. Keep ahead a short distance for a fine view of the picturesque Donington Mill but the route continues along the road to the left to return to the start. •

The mill at Donington on Bain

Woodhall Spa

Start	Woodhall Spa
Distance	6½ miles (10.5km)
Approximate time	3 hours
Parking	Woodhall Spa
Refreshments	Pubs and cafés at Woodhall Spa
Ordnance Survey maps	Explorer 273 (Lincolnshire Wolds South), Landranger 122 (Skegness & Horncastle)

A pleasant opening stretch along the Viking Way, across fields and by woodland, is followed by quiet roads and lanes. You rejoin the Viking Way for the last 1½ miles (2.4km), which is mainly through the beautiful pine and birch woodlands that surround Woodhall Spa, making an excellent finale to the walk.

Woodhall Spa developed as a small health resort in the Victorian period, when a pump room and hotels were built, but it declined after World War I. Now it is a popular golfing and walking centre. In World War II it had associations with the Dambusters, and there is a memorial to them in the town centre.

Start at the crossroads in the town centre and walk along Witham Road, signposted to Martin and Lincoln. After ½ mile (800m) – just after crossing Wentworth Way – turn right Ⓐ, at a public footpath sign, along an enclosed path. Follow this path through new housing areas to a narrow lane, turn

A path through woodland near Woodhall Spa

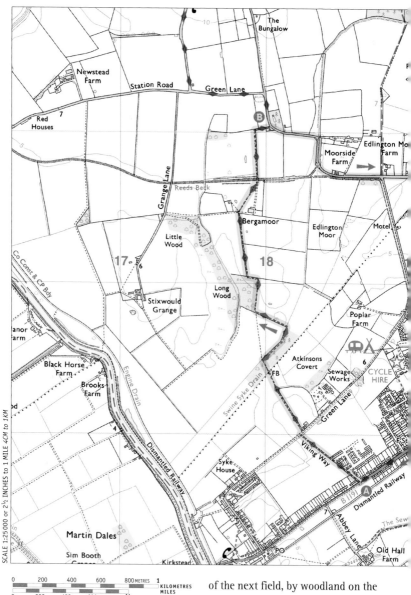

right and almost immediately turn left along a straight track across fields. After crossing a drain and track, keep ahead through woodland and, on emerging from the trees, turn right along the right-hand edge of a field. In the field corner, turn left and, at a public footpath sign, turn right over a stile and walk along the left-hand edge of the next field, by woodland on the left. At the corner of the trees, turn left and, at the next public footpath sign, turn right and walk straight across a field. On the far side cross a track, climb a stile, bear right and head diagonally across the next field, making for a waymarked post in front of a brick bridge.

Cross the bridge over Reeds Beck, keep ahead to climb a stile and continue along the right-hand edge of a field.

In the corner, turn right over another stile and walk along an enclosed track to a road **B**. Turn right, follow the road around first a right- and then a left-hand bend and, where it bends right again, keep ahead along a straight, tree-lined, narrow lane to a T-junction **C**. Turn left, passing a monument to the Duke of Wellington on the left, and take the first lane on the right **D**.

After almost 1 mile (1.6km) – just after entering trees – turn right **E**, at a public footpath sign, to a kissing-gate and keep ahead through woodland. At a T-junction, turn right on to a path which crosses part of a golf course and continues through this delightful woodland back to Woodhall Spa. The track eventually becomes a tarmac one which reaches a road **F**.

Turn left through a gate, walk along a tarmac path and go through another gate. Keep ahead to a T-junction and turn right to the start. ●

Bourne Wood and Edenham

Start	Bourne
Distance	6½ miles (10.5km)
Approximate time	3 hours
Parking	Bourne
Refreshments	Pubs and cafés at Bourne, pub at Edenham
Ordnance Survey maps	Explorer 248 (Bourne & Heckington), Landranger 130 (Grantham)

A short and pleasant stroll from the town centre of Bourne leads to the edge of Bourne Wood. After emerging from the wood, the route continues down into the East Glen valley to the village of Edenham. The return leg takes you through the wood again. Apart from attractive woodland walking, there are grand and extensive views across the East Glen valley to the limestone hills of south-west Lincolnshire and the route is well waymarked throughout.

Bourne is one of a number of places around the Fens claimed to be the birthplace of the legendary Hereward the Wake, leader of the last Saxon revolt against the Norman conquerors. The mainly 12th-century church was once part of an abbey, founded in 1138. After the dissolution of the monasteries by Henry VIII, the nave, which had been used by the local townspeople, continued in use as the parish church.

The walk begins at the crossroads in the town centre. Facing the town hall (built in 1821), turn left along North Street and, after ¼ mile (400m), turn left **A** along a tarmac track (Christopher's Lane), which bears left. Where the tarmac ends, keep ahead to a public footpath sign and turn right to continue along an enclosed path to a road. Turn left to a T-junction, turn right along a road (Beech Avenue) that curves left and, at a public footpath sign, turn right along an enclosed path.

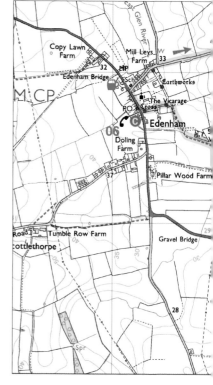

At the next public footpath sign, turn left to continue along a narrow path – between garden fences on the left and a drain on the right – cross a road, keep ahead and, after climbing a stile, the route continues along the right-hand edge of two fields. In the corner of the second field, climb a stile to enter Bourne Wood and keep ahead to a T-junction. This beautiful area of mixed woodland has a sculpture trail, and some of the pieces are passed on the route.

At the T-junction, turn right along a straight track, turn left **Ⓑ** at a public footpath sign, keep ahead at a cross-roads and climb a stile to emerge from the trees. Bear left along the left-hand edge of a field, go through a hedge gap and keep ahead. The next hedge gap reveals a superb view ahead over the East Glen valley, with the tower of Edenham church below and Grimsthorpe Castle on the horizon. After going through the gap, turn left along the left-hand field edge and, at a way-marked post, follow the path to the right, walking downhill into the valley, still keeping by the left-hand edge of a field.

Look out for where a waymarked post directs you to turn left through a hedge gap and turn right to continue gently

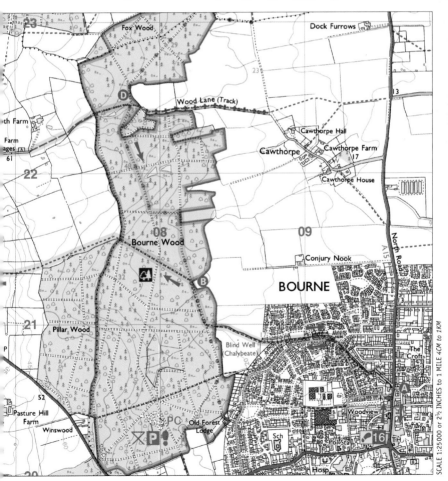

The East Glen valley near Edenham

downhill along the right-hand edge of a field. Cross a bridge over the East Glen River and immediately turn right through a hedge gap to walk along the riverbank. Follow the river around a left-hand bend and, at a public footpath sign, turn right to cross a bridge over it. Bear left, head diagonally across a field to the far left-hand corner, where you join a track, keep ahead to a lane and turn left to a road **C**.

Turn right into Edenham, passing to the left of the 13th-century church. Its tall Perpendicular tower is a prominent landmark for miles around. Just before the Five Bells pub, turn right along School Lane, signposted to Bulby and Morton. Where the road bends left,

keep ahead along a lane, climbing steadily out of the valley. Where the lane ends, keep ahead along a track signposted to Cawthorpe and, where the track bends right, continue along the right-hand edge of two fields. In the corner of the second field, go through a gate to re-enter Bourne Wood. Take the path ahead and, on reaching a well-surfaced track, turn right **D**.

The track later descends to a crossroads, where you turn left along a track signposted Lincolnshire Cycle Way. At a T-junction, turn right and after passing a public footpath sign **B**, you pick up the outward route and retrace your steps back to the starting point. ●

Chapel St Leonards, Hogsthorpe and Chapel Point

Start	Chapel St Leonards
Distance	7 miles (11.3km)
Approximate time	3½ hours
Parking	Chapel St Leonards
Refreshments	Pubs and cafés at Chapel St Leonards, pubs at Hogsthorpe, pub and café at Chapel Point
Ordnance Survey maps	Explorer 274 (Skegness, Alford & Spilsby), Landranger 122 (Skegness & Horncastle)

From the coast at Chapel St Leonards, the route first heads inland across fields to Hogsthorpe. It continues across reclaimed marshland, using a combination of tracks, field paths and quiet lanes, to return to the coast at Wolla Bank. A final stretch of just under 2 miles (3.2km) along a sandy beach, passing the slight promontory of Chapel Point, leads back to the start.

Start by the large green in the village centre and walk along Sea Road, signposted to Hogsthorpe and Skegness. After crossing a bridge over Orby Drain, turn left **A** along Church Lane and follow it around a right-hand bend to where it ends .

Keep ahead along the right-hand edge of a churchyard, passing St Leonard's Church, built in 1794 and extended in the Victorian period. Turn right over a stile, turn left along the left-hand edge of a field, climb two stiles in quick succession and continue along the left-hand edge of the next two fields. In the corner of the second field, climb a stile, cross a foot-bridge over a drain and walk along the left-hand field edge above the drain. After crossing another drain, keep

The church at Chapel St Leonards

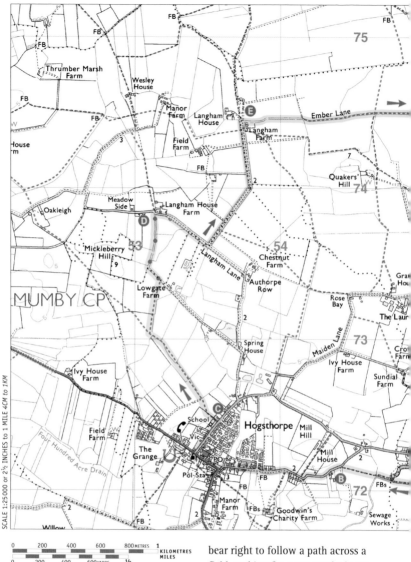

SCALE 1:25 000 or 2½ INCHES to 1 MILE 4CM to 1KM

0	200	400	600	800 METRES	1
					KILOMETRES
					MILES
0	200	400	600 YARDS	½	

ahead across the next field to emerge on to a lane **B**.

Turn left along the winding lane into Hogsthorpe. At a T-junction, turn right and turn right again, by the medieval church and Saracens Head, into Thames Street. At a public footpath sign, turn left **C** along an enclosed track, go through a gate and continue along the right-hand edge of a playing-field. Go through a kissing-gate in the corner,

bear right to follow a path across a field, making for a waymarked post, and continue along the left-hand field edge. After crossing a footbridge, keep along the right-hand field edge and, in the corner, turn first left and then turn right to cross a footbridge over a drain.

Walk along the right-hand edge of a field, cross a footbridge, keep along the left-hand edge of the next field and, after the next footbridge, you reach a fork. Turn right to continue along the right-hand edge of two fields above a drain. At the next waymarked post,

keep straight ahead across the field and, on the far side, cross a footbridge and turn left along a track. The track bends right to a lane **D**.

Turn right, take the first lane on the left and, after just over ¹⁄₂ mile (800m) – in front of the gate to Langham House – turn right along a track **E**.

Follow this track – Ember Lane – for 1¹⁄₄ miles (2km), eventually reaching a road by Bank Farm Country Club **F**.

Turn left and, where the road bends left, turn right along a tarmac drive, signposted to Wolla Bank. Keep ahead through the car park and picnic area and head over the dunes to the beach **G**.

Turn right and walk along the beach to Chapel Point, where concrete steps appear **H**.

This promontory was part of the east coast defences during World War II, and the gun platform is still there. From here you can either continue along the beach or along a tarmac track above it to Chapel St Leonards. Where you see a road on the right, turn along it to return to the starting point. ●

Old Bolingbroke and East Keal

Start	Old Bolingbroke
Distance	6½ miles (10.5km)
Approximate time	3½ hours
Parking	Roadside parking at Old Bolingbroke
Refreshments	Pub at Old Bolingbroke
Ordnance Survey maps	Explorer 273 (Lincolnshire Wolds South), Landranger 122 (Skegness & Horncastle)

The route takes you over the gentle slopes of the wolds that lie between the attractive villages of Old Bolingbroke and East Keal. There are wide and sweeping views and, as this is a walk on the south-eastern fringes of the wolds, these views extend southwards across the Fens to Boston Stump and eastwards to the North Sea coast. Historic interest is provided by the castle ruins and church at Old Bolingbroke.

Old Bolingbroke is a place of faded glories. Nowadays it is hard to envisage this small and sleepy village as a centre of royal power but in medieval times Bolingbroke Castle was a seat of the powerful House of Lancaster and the birthplace in 1366 of Henry IV, first of the Lancastrian kings. The 13th-century castle is a meagre if atmospheric ruin, comprising little more than a few low outer walls and part of the gatehouse. It declined in the Tudor period and was destroyed after the Civil War. The nearby 14th-century church is just the south aisle of a much larger structure, about three times its present size, probably built by John of Gaunt, father of Henry IV. It also suffered damage during the Civil War.

Start by the war memorial in the village centre and walk along the narrow lane beside the Black Horse pub, which passes between the church on the left and castle ruins on the right. Follow the winding lane to a crossroads, keep ahead along the lane signposted to East Keal and West Keal, at a fork take the right-hand lane and bear left on joining another lane Ⓐ. The lane heads over Keal Hill and, at a fork at the top, continue along the left-hand lane, climbing more gently to a T-junction Ⓑ. The tower of West Keal church is seen across the fields on the right, and the views extend across the Fens to Boston Stump on the horizon.

At the T-junction, climb the stile opposite, immediately turn right through a gate and walk diagonally across a field to a stile on the far side. Climb it and, as you continue in the same direction across the next field, you are looking across the coastal plain to the North Sea. Make for a footpath post by a hedge gap, go through the gap and head downhill across a field to a waymarked post in the trees on the far side. Keep ahead through the belt of trees, climb a stile, continue gently downhill across the next field and climb a stile on to a track.

Turn right and, where the track bends left, keep ahead over a stile and through a gate onto a road in East Keal Ⓒ. Turn left, take the second lane on the right (Church Lane) and follow it around a left-hand bend to the medieval church, heavily restored in the 19th century. Just before the church, turn left at a public footpath sign, along an enclosed path that enters a field and continue across it, passing beside a gate in the far corner onto a road Ⓓ.

Cross over, take the lane opposite, signposted to Old Bolingbroke and Mavis Enderby, which heads gently uphill, follow it around a left-hand bend and, at a public footpath sign, turn

| 0 | 200 | 400 | 600 | 800 METRES | 1 |
| 0 | 200 | 400 | 600 YARDS | ½ | KILOMETRES MILES |

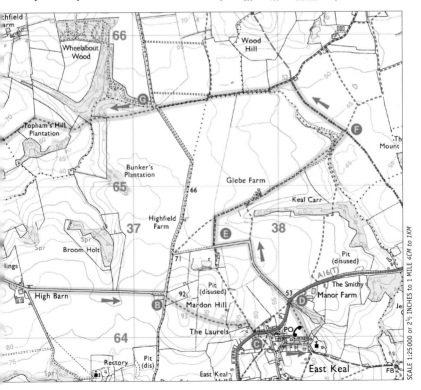

SCALE 1:25000 or 2½ INCHES to 1 MILE 4CM to 1KM

Wolds scenery near Old Bolingbroke

right along the track to Glebe Farm **E**. The track bends right and, at a fork in front of a barn, take the right-hand track, passing beside a metal barrier. Descend gently into a dip and, just after passing through a belt of trees, turn left **F** at a crossing of paths and tracks. At the next crossways, to the left of a barn, turn left on to a track along the right-hand edge of a field. The track narrows to a path, which keeps along the left-hand edge of the next field and then widens into a track again and continues across more fields.

Look out for a yellow-waymarked post, where you bear left on to a path that continues in a straight line across the field and goes through a hedge gap onto a lane. Turn right and, at a public footpath sign, turn left **G** along a track, which runs parallel to the right-hand edge of a field. Before reaching the field

corner, bear left across to a public footpath sign, keep ahead through a wide hedge gap and head downhill to cross a footbridge on the far side of the field.

Climb a stile, head gently uphill across the next field, join a track on the far side and continue along it over the brow. At a public footpath sign, turn left and walk along the right-hand edge of the next two fields. At a hedge corner, continue across to the far side and then keep ahead along a narrow path through an area of scrub and rough grass, by a wire fence on the left. On emerging into a field, bear slightly left across it, looking out for a waymarked kissing-gate.

Go through, head quite steeply downhill and go through another kissing-gate on to a lane. Turn left and follow the lane around a left curve into Old Bolingbroke. At a junction, turn right, in the Asgarby and Hareby direction, to return to the start. ●

Lincoln and the Fossdyke

Start	Lincoln, tourist information centre
Distance	7½ miles (12.1km)
Approximate time	3½ hours
Parking	Lincoln
Refreshments	Pubs and cafés at Lincoln, pub where the route leaves the Fossdyke
Ordnance Survey maps	Explorer 272 (Lincoln), Landranger 121 (Lincoln & Newark-on-Trent)

This figure-of-eight walk gives you the opportunity to combine many of the splendid historic and architectural treasures of Lincoln, one of England's foremost historic cities, with the pleasant countryside that lies at the foot of Lincoln Edge to the west of it. After descending from the edge, most of the route is beside the waterways of the Fossdyke and adjacent drainage channels. For much of the way the views are dominated by the towering presence of Lincoln Cathedral, and the final ½ mile (800m) is a steep climb to the cathedral and castle, one of the finest urban walks in the country.

Lincoln was founded as a fortress, and later a city, by the Romans at the point where the River Witham cuts through the limestone ridge of Lincoln Edge, and the city possesses one of only two surviving Roman gateways in England, the Newport Arch.

Dominating the city and much of the surrounding countryside is the majestic cathedral. The diocese was established here by the Normans in 1073, and the first cathedral was begun soon afterwards. This was almost totally destroyed by an earthquake in 1185, and the subsequent rebuilding, mainly carried out between 1192 and 1280 by a succession of energetic bishops, produced one of Europe's Gothic masterpieces. The whole of the exterior is rich in detail, and the west front is particularly awe-inspiring, a huge 13th-century screen grafted on to some of the 12th-century arches of the original Norman cathedral. The interior is spacious and dignified and is noted for the beautiful late-13th-century Angel Choir, which was the last part of the main body of the church to be constructed, and for the intricate carvings of the choir stalls.

Next to the cathedral is the castle, founded by William the Conqueror in 1068. The curtain walls, gateways and some of the towers survive from the medieval castle but other structures date from the 18th and 19th centuries and include law courts and prison buildings. There is also a fascinating Magna Carta exhibition. Just to the south of the cathedral are the ruins of the medieval bishop's palace, also worth a visit.

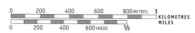 The walk begins at the top of Steep Hill and, with the castle on your left and the cathedral on your right, walk along Bailgate, passing to the right of the tourist information centre.

Turn left into Westgate to continue alongside the castle wall, at a T-junction turn right into Burton Road but almost immediately turn left along an enclosed tarmac path. The path bends right and continues to a road. Turn left downhill to a T-junction, turn left into Yarborough Road and, just after passing Long Leys Road, turn right, at a public footpath sign, along an enclosed tarmac path **A**.

The path heads downhill along the left-hand edge of West Common (or Carholme), one of the open spaces around the city, to a main road. Cross over, continue along the left-hand edge of Carholme Golf Course to reach the Fossdyke and turn right alongside it **B**. This canal can claim to be the oldest in the country as it was originally cut by

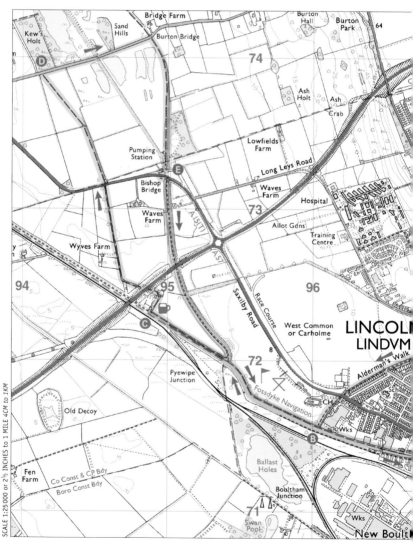

the Romans around AD 120 to link the River Witham at Lincoln with the River Trent.

Cross a footbridge over Catchwater Drain, continue by the Fossdyke as far as the Pyewipe Inn and, at a public bridleway sign, turn right alongside the pub . Walk through the car park and continue along a tarmac drive, which bends left to pass under a main road, then bends right and keeps in a straight line to a road. Cross over and walk along the right-hand edge of a field. Turn left in the corner, turn right to go through a hedge gap and over a drain, turn right again and turn left to continue along the right-hand edge of the next field. After about 50 yds (46m), bear left and head diagonally across the field to a road ⒟.

Turn right, cross a bridge over Main Drain, keep ahead to the next bridge and turn right, at a public bridleway sign, on to a path that keeps above the right bank of Catchwater Drain. Now follows a most attractive part of the walk: the drain is partially tree-lined and there are views across the fields to the left of Lincoln Edge and the cathedral towers. At a T-junction, turn

Steep Hill, Lincoln

right to cross a bridge over Main Drain, and the track curves left to a road. Turn left, recross the drain and, at a public footpath sign, turn right over a stile ⒠ and continue along an embankment between the two drains. Pass under a road bridge and, just after climbing a stile, you reach the Fossdyke again.

Turn left over a footbridge – here temporarily rejoining the outward route – walk beside the Fossdyke but, at a public footpath sign ⒝, leave the outward route by continuing beside the canal. You keep beside the Fossdyke all the while into Lincoln, alternately along paths and roads and finally passing under a bridge to reach a road. Turn right to keep along the north side of Brayford Pool, once an inland port surrounded by warehouses and now a marina with hotels, a cinema complex and university buildings. Pass under a bridge to continue beside the River Witham and go up steps beside the High Bridge to emerge into High Street ⒡.

Turn left, pass under the medieval Stonebow and keep ahead up the hill – first along High Street, then the Strait and finally the aptly named Steep Hill (it gets progressively steeper) to return to the start. On the way, you pass a variety of attractive old buildings, including two rare examples of 12th-century houses, and catch tantalising glimpses of the cathedral towers. ●

Long Sutton and South Holland Main Drain

Long Sutton and South Holland Main Drain

Start	Long Sutton
Distance	7½ miles (12.1km)
Approximate time	3½ hours
Parking	Long Sutton
Refreshments	Pubs and café at Long Sutton
Ordnance Survey maps	Explorers 249 (Spalding & Holbeach) and 235 (Wisbech & Peterborough North), Landranger 131 (Boston & Spalding)

This invigorating walk to the south of the Wash takes you along field paths, tracks and quiet lanes, and there are wide and extensive views across the surrounding flat, fenland landscape. About halfway round, there is a 1¼-mile (2km) stretch along the north bank of South Holland Main Drain, which is part of the complex drainage system of the Fens.

The walk starts at the top end of the market place by Long Sutton's large and imposing church, one of the finest in a county of outstanding churches. It is particularly noted for its 13th-century tower – originally detached – which is topped by one of the earliest lead spires in England, and its impressive Norman nave.

At a public footpath sign take the paved path through the churchyard, passing to the right of the church. Go through gates on to a road, turn left and, after about 50 yds (46m), turn right at a public footpath sign, along an enclosed tarmac path that continues across a park to a road **A**. Cross over to a public footpath sign opposite, walk along an enclosed and paved path, pass through a hedge gap and turn right along the right-hand edge of fields. At a waymarked footbridge, turn right to cross a dyke and turn left to continue along the left-hand edge of a field. In the corner, cross a footbridge over another dyke, turn right and then almost immediately left and walk along the right-hand edge of a field. At a waymarked post, turn left to a tarmac track, turn right to a T-junction and turn right **B** along a narrow lane (Hospital Drove). After 1 mile (1.6km) you reach a T-junction. Keep ahead along a track to the busy A17, cross carefully, walk along the track opposite, which emerges on to a lane, and continue along this to the South Holland Main Drain **C**. Turn right beside it – keeping below an embankment – cross a road to the right of a bridge and continue beside the drain to a fork.

Take the right-hand path that climbs

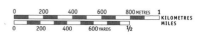

the embankment to the corner of a lane  D and turn right along it (Sea Bank). Turn left at a T-junction, and the lane curves right to another T-junction. Turn left again, at the next T-junction turn right and, at the next one, turn right again along Tydd Low Road. Ignore the first public footpath sign on the right but at the next one – just after passing St James Road on the left – turn right E along the right-hand edge of a field. After crossing a dyke, turn left alongside it, curving first left and then right, and carefully recross the A17. Walk along the left-hand edge of a field above a dyke and, where the dyke bends right, cross a footbridge over it.

Bear right along a path that heads across fields directly towards Long Sutton church and look out for where a yellow-waymarked post directs you to turn left. At the next waymarked post, turn right along a path and, on entering a field, bear left along its left-hand edge. After the edge curves right, follow the path to the left, by a brick wall on the right.

Cross a footbridge and continue along an enclosed path, which emerges on to a road. Keep ahead to a T-junction and turn right to return to the start. ●

South Holland Main Drain

Southrey, Bardney and Tupholme Abbey

Start	Southrey, car park at end of Ferry Road
Distance	8½ miles (13.7km)
Approximate time	4 hours
Parking	Southrey
Refreshments	Pub at Southrey, pubs at Bardney
Ordnance Survey maps	Explorer 273 (Lincolnshire Wolds South), Landranger 121 (Lincoln & Newark-on-Trent)

There is much interest and variety on this walk on the edge of the Fens. It begins by the banks of the River Witham at Southrey and takes you across fields and by woodlands to the village of Bardney. Historic interest is provided by the churches at Southrey and Bardney and the sites of the now almost vanished medieval abbeys of Bardney and Tupholme. This is an easy and well-waymarked route with clear paths and tracks, and there is a succession of wide views.

The car park by the River Witham is on the site of the former Southrey station.

🖊 Begin by walking along the road, passing the Riverside Inn and tiny, white-painted, wooden church. The church, built in 1898, looks as if it belongs more to New England than the edge of the Lincolnshire fens.

At a Viking Way sign, turn left Ⓐ along Highthorpe, follow the narrow lane around a right-hand bend and, at a T-junction, turn left. Where the lane peters out by a farm, keep ahead along a track that bends right. At a T-junction, turn right along the right-hand edge of a field, follow it to the left and continue along the left-hand edge of Southrey Wood. Beyond the corner of the wood, the track continues across fields, and the views are dominated by the sugar factory on the left and the houses and church tower of Bardney on the right.

On approaching the village, turn right at a public footpath sign Ⓑ, along an enclosed path, which bends left on to a road. Turn right along the road, passing to the left of the church, into the village centre. The 15th-century church, an attractive mixture of stone and brick, was built after the earlier church by the abbey collapsed in 1431. Some of the stones in the nave came from the abbey and some of the bricks in the chancel from Tattershall Castle.

Turn left, at a T-junction turn left again Ⓒ along Abbey Road and follow it to Abbey Farm. The mounds seen in the field ahead are all that remains of Bardney Abbey and these can be inspected more closely by keeping ahead to the parking area. The original 7th-century abbey, founded by Ethelred of Mercia, was destroyed by the Vikings in 870 and refounded by the Normans in 1087. After its dissolution by Henry VIII in the 1530s, the buildings were demolished and all that is visible on the site are some earthworks and grass-covered mounds.

At a public bridleway sign, turn right Ⓓ along a straight track by the right-hand edge of fields, later continuing across fields. At a fingerpost, keep ahead – here leaving the Viking Way – to a road. Turn right and, at a public bridleway sign, turn left Ⓔ along a wide grassy track, later keeping by the right-hand edge of Scotgrove Wood, to a stile. Climb it, walk along the left-hand edge of a field, parallel to a farm track, and look out for where you go through a gate to continue along the track to a road.

Cross over and take the tarmac track opposite, which curves right. After passing between a house and barn, it becomes a rough track. The track curves first left, then right and heads towards a farm. At a waymarked post to the left of the farm buildings, turn left Ⓕ along the left-hand edge of a field, cross a plank footbridge over a ditch and continue across the next field, making for a waymarked stile on the far side. Climb it, continue across the next field, climb another stile, in the far right-hand corner, and turn right along a narrow lane. Ahead, the ruins of Tupholme Abbey can be seen.

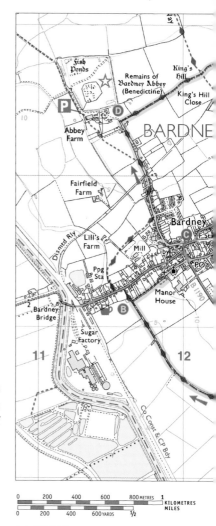

Remains of Tupholme Abbey

At a T-junction, turn right along a road and, where it bends right, turn left Ⓖ through a kissing-gate and walk along a track, passing to the right of the abbey. This was a small monastic house, founded in the 12th century by Premonstratensian canons. There is slightly more here than at Bardney – part of the south wall of the refectory.

The track later becomes hedge-lined and continues to a T-junction Ⓗ. Turn right – here rejoining the Viking Way – and follow a track past a farm and over a footbridge to eventually emerge on to a road in Southrey. Turn left to return to the start. ●

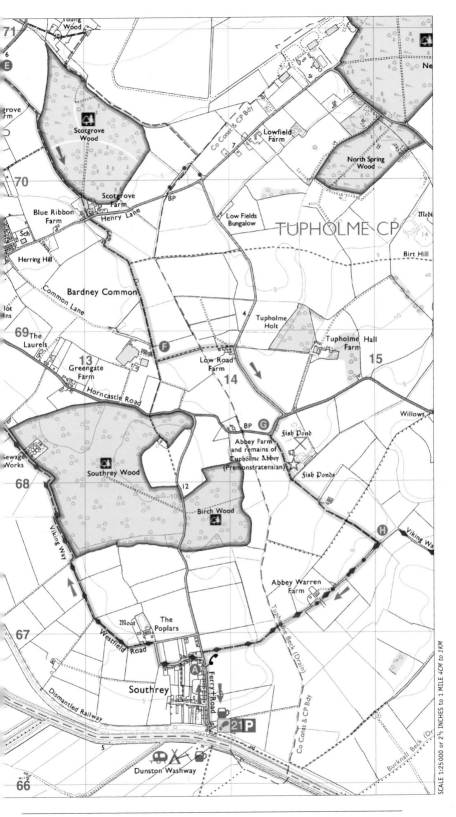

SCALE 1:25000 or 2½ INCHES to 1 MILE 4CM to 1KM

Crowland and the River Welland

Start	Crowland
Distance	8½ miles (13.7km)
Approximate time	4 hours
Parking	Crowland, North Street
Refreshments	Pubs and cafés at Crowland, pub by Fen Bridge
Ordnance Survey maps	Explorer 235 (Wisbech & Peterborough North), Landranger 131 (Boston & Spalding)

Almost the whole of this exhilarating walk is along embankments above either the River Welland or the parallel New River Drain. It is an entirely flat walk across a typical fenland landscape, where the views seem to stretch for ever. For most of the return leg, the tower and spire of Crowland Abbey are in sight.

The remains of Crowland (or Croyland) Abbey give some indication of the magnificence of what was one of the greatest of fenland monasteries. Particularly impressive is the ornate, partially ruined west front. Originally founded by King Ethelbald of Mercia for St Guthlac in 716, the abbey had an eventful history, being plundered, burnt and rebuilt several times. It was dissolved by Henry VIII in the 1530s, and the west front and nave of the church are the main surviving portions. The north aisle is used as the parish church.

The town grew up around the abbey and, until the draining of the Fens, the rivers ran along the main streets. This is why the streets are so wide. It also explains the presence of the unique Trinity (or Triangular) Bridge in the town centre, an impressive piece of 14th-century engineering that is now redundant. It was built at a junction of two rivers, and its three arches spanned all the channels.

Start by Trinity Bridge at the junction of North, South, East and West Streets and walk along North Street, passing some thatched buildings and a series of greens. At a T-junction, turn left **A**, follow the road around a left-hand curve and turn right along the road signposted to Deeping St James and Market Deeping. Walk along the grass verge – it is a public footpath and there are a succession of footbridges – and over to the left is 'The Lake', all that remains of a channel cut to link the town with the River Welland. It is now a picnic area.

At Fen Bridge turn right over a stile **B** and continue along an embankment above the River Welland, negotiating several stiles and gates. The views across the Fens from here are tremendous and there is not a trace of a hill in sight. After 3½ miles (5.6km) you reach

0	200	400	600	800 METRES	1
					KILOMETRES
					MILES
0	200	400	600 YARDS	½

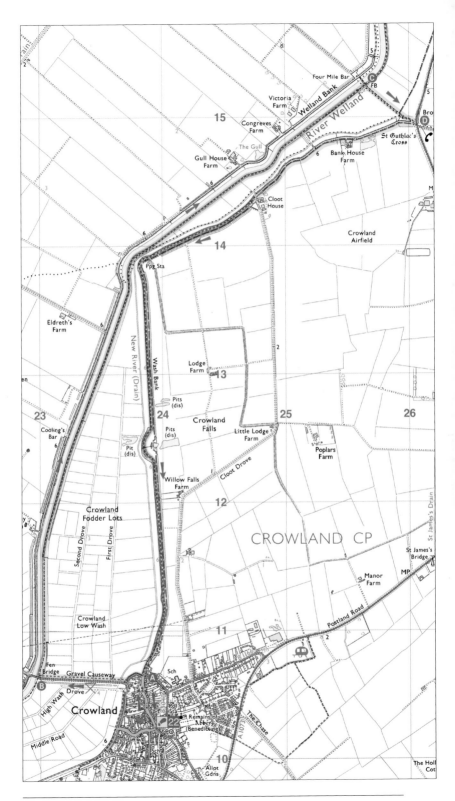

a footbridge over the river. Turn right ⓒ to descend the embankment and walk along a track, going round first right- and then left-hand bends. Cross the New River Drain and keep ahead to a lane near where it joins a road.

Turn sharp right ⓓ along the narrow lane, passing the remains of St Guthlac's Cross, and, where it bends left, keep ahead along an embankment to a stile. After climbing it, you keep along the embankment (Wash Bank) above the New River Drain back to Crowland. There are several stiles, and for most of the way the tower and short spire of the abbey are in view. Finally, climb a stile onto a track on the edge of the town, keep ahead to a road, cross over and walk along North Street to return to the starting point. ●

The west front of Crowland Abbey

Barnetby le Wold, Bigby and Somerby

Start	Barnetby le Wold
Distance	7½ miles (12.1km)
Approximate time	3½ hours
Parking	Roadside parking at Barnetby le Wold in main street near the post office
Refreshments	Pubs at Barnetby le Wold
Ordnance Survey maps	Explorer 281 (Ancholme Valley), Landranger 112 (Scunthorpe & Gainsborough)

The route follows the Viking Way southwards from Barnetby le Wold, passing through the hamlets of Bigby and Somerby, before heading up onto the gentle, fresh and open slopes of the northern wolds. The extensive views from here include the Ancholme valley to the west and extend to the industries of Humberside on the eastern horizon.

Barnetby le Wold is mainly a creation of the Victorian railway era, situated at the junction of three lines, but the semi-derelict Norman church on the south side of the village is evidence of an older agricultural settlement.

🖉 Start in the main street by the post office and, facing it, turn right and take the first road on the right (St Mary's Avenue). Just before the road ends, turn right onto a tarmac track, which soon becomes a rough, fence-lined track. The first part of the walk follows the well-waymarked Viking Way. At a crossing of paths and tracks Ⓐ, keep ahead along an enclosed path that continues in a straight line across fields to a narrow lane. Turn left and, where the lane curves left, turn right Ⓑ at a public footpath sign, along an enclosed track.

The track heads in a straight line across fields and, where it ends, bear slightly left on to a faint path across a field to a footbridge on the far side. Cross it, keep ahead across the next field to a T-junction, turn right and, at a waymarked post, turn left to continue along the right-hand edge of a field. Bear left on meeting a track, turn left at a T-junction and, at a public footpath sign, turn right along the right-hand edge of a field. In the corner, cross a footbridge over a ditch, turn right to cross another one and turn left along the left-hand edge of the next field.

Follow the track around a left-hand bend to a T-junction, turn right along a tarmac lane and follow the lane around a left-hand bend to another T-junction, in the hamlet of Bigby Ⓒ. The 13th-century church is to the left. Turn right along a road and, at a T-junction, keep ahead through a gate and walk across a field to a stile on the far side. Climb it, cross a plank footbridge, climb another

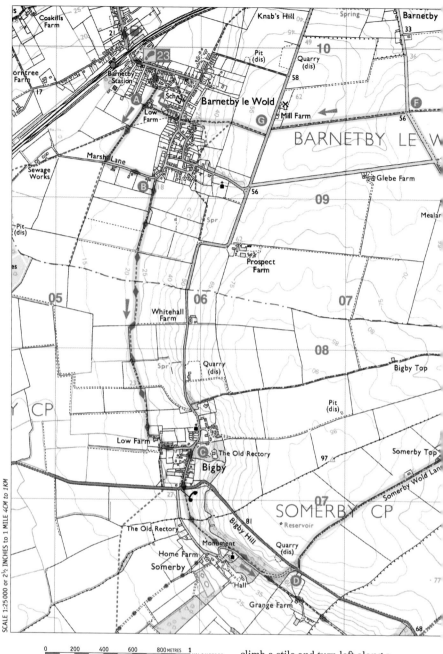

SCALE 1:25 000 or 2½ INCHES to 1 MILE 4CM to 1KM

```
0    200   400   600   800 METRES   1
                                    KILOMETRES
                                    MILES
0    200   400   600 YARDS   ½
```

stile and bear slightly left uphill towards a monument. This was built in 1770 to commemorate 29 years of marriage between Sir Edward and Ann Weston of Somerby Hall.

Continue beyond the monument to climb a stile and turn left along a narrow, wooded lane, passing to the left of Somerby's small medieval church. The west tower is scarcely higher than the roof. At a fork, continue along the left-hand lane – here leaving the Viking Way – which curves left gently uphill through trees to a crossroads **D**. Take the lane ahead, signposted to Somerby

Wolds near Barnetby

hand one of the two footpath posts seen in front – and continue along the right-hand edge of a field. In the corner, turn left to keep along the right-hand edge, go through a hedge gap and, at a T-junction, turn sharp left along an enclosed track **E**. Follow this broad, undulating track to a T-junction, turn right and continue along the track for just over $^1/_2$ mile (800m) to join a tarmac track. Keep ahead to emerge on to a lane at a corner, continue ahead and, where the lane bears right, turn left **F** at a public footpath sign, along the left-hand edge of a field. Climb a stile, keep along the left-hand edge of the next field, climb another stile and turn left along a road. At a public footpath sign, turn right **G** along the left-hand edge of a field, heading gently downhill towards Barnetby in the shallow valley below.

Climb a stile, continue downhill to climb another one and keep ahead along a track between houses to a road. Take the tarmac track opposite, pass beside a gate and continue along the track to a crossroads **A**. Turn right, here rejoining the outward route, and retrace your steps to the start. ●

Top, which heads over Somerby Wold. Beyond Somerby Top Farm, it continues as a rough track and, where it bends right, keep ahead, at a public bridleway sign, along the right-hand edge of a field.

On entering a field, bear slightly left across it, making for another public bridleway sign at a corner – the right-

Around Horncastle

Start	Horncastle
Distance	9 miles (14.5km)
Approximate time	4½ hours
Parking	Horncastle
Refreshments	Pubs and cafés at Horncastle, pub by Shearman's Wath Bridge
Ordnance Survey maps	Explorer 273 (Lincolnshire Wolds South), Landranger 122 (Skegness & Horncastle)

The walk is a lengthy and wide circuit of the Bain valley to the north, west and south of Horncastle, and the first and last parts are along the Viking Way. It is a mainly flat walk at the base of the wolds, and the views westwards extend to the long ridge of Lincoln Edge, with the towers of Lincoln Cathedral visible on the horizon. The final stretch is a relaxing stroll beside the Horncastle Canal. Expect mud in some places after wet weather.

Horncastle is situated on the site of a Roman fort, and there are a few remaining fragments of the Roman walls, one of which is incorporated into the structure of the library. Nowadays the town is renowned as an antiques centre. The church, built from the local greenstone, dates mainly from the 12th and 13th centuries, though it was heavily restored in Victorian times.

Start in the Market Place and, with your back to the post office, turn left. At a crossroads keep ahead along Banks Street – later walking beside the little River Waring – and at a Viking Way sign turn left into Linden Road. Take the first road on the right, at a crossroads keep ahead along Bowl Alley Lane and, where the road bends left, keep ahead along an enclosed track. At a public footpath sign, turn left Ⓐ to continue along an enclosed path and the go through a kissing-gate onto a lane.

Turn right, take the first lane on the left (signposted to Fulletby) and, after ½ mile (800m), turn left Ⓑ at a public bridleway sign, along a track. Turn right in front of a gate to walk along the left-hand edge of a field, pass through a gap into the next field and turn left along its left-hand edge. At a Viking Way sign, turn right by the right-hand edge of a ditch, later crossing the ditch to continue along its left-hand edge to a T-junction. Turn left Ⓒ – here leaving the Viking Way – along a broad track that ascends gently to the A153 just to the south of West Ashby.

Cross carefully and continue along the lane opposite for 1½ miles (2.4km), passing the Golfers Arms public house and crossing the River Bain to reach the busy A158 Ⓓ. Again cross carefully and take the track opposite across fields, later keeping along the left-hand edge of woodland. At a public bridle-

The Horncastle Canal

way sign, where the edge of the wood bears right, keep straight ahead across the field to a footpath post on the far side Ⓔ and turn left along a path, passing along the left-hand edge of a solitary clump of trees. Keep straight ahead across the field towards the houses of Thimbleby, making for a footbridge over a ditch, cross it and continue to a stile on the far side. After

climbing it, keep ahead along a tarmac path and then a road to a T-junction in the village of Thimbleby Ⓕ.

This attractive village has some thatched cottages in the main street and a Victorian church at its eastern end. Take the tarmac track opposite and, after crossing a track, keep straight ahead across a field to a yellow-waymarked post just to the left of a hedge corner. Cross a footbridge, walk along the right-hand edge of a field and, at a hedge corner, continue across the field and climb a stile on to a lane.

Turn right into the hamlet of Langton, passing to the left of the tiny 19th-century church and, at the entrance to Langton Manor Farm, turn left **G** along an enclosed path to a stile. Climb it, walk first along an enclosed path, then across grass parallel to a track on the left and climb a stile to continue along that track. After going through a hedge gap, the track bends left but the right-of-way keeps straight ahead across a field, crosses a ditch and continues across the next field, passing to the left of a tree to rejoin the track. Turn right along it to a lane, keep ahead to a road **H** and turn left into the hamlet of Thornton. Another small church can be seen to the left.

Where the road bends left, keep ahead along a narrow lane – there is a fine view ahead of the wolds – and, after crossing a bridge over the Horncastle Canal, turn left **J** over a stile, here rejoining the Viking Way for the last part of the walk. It is an attractive and relaxing finale as you follow a grassy path across meadows beside the canal back to Horncastle. In the far corner of the meadows, go through a kissing-gate, keep beside the canal to join a tarmac path, follow the path around a right-hand bend and cross a footbridge over the River Bain.

Continue beside the canal along the left-hand edge of a sports field and turn left **K** to cross first a bridge over the canal and then a road. Keep ahead along a paved path between attractive old cottages into St Mary's Square to the church and bear right to return to the Market Place.

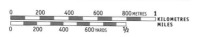

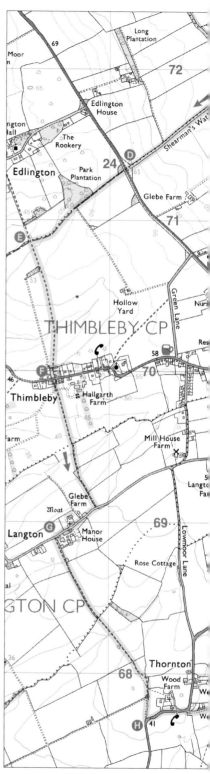

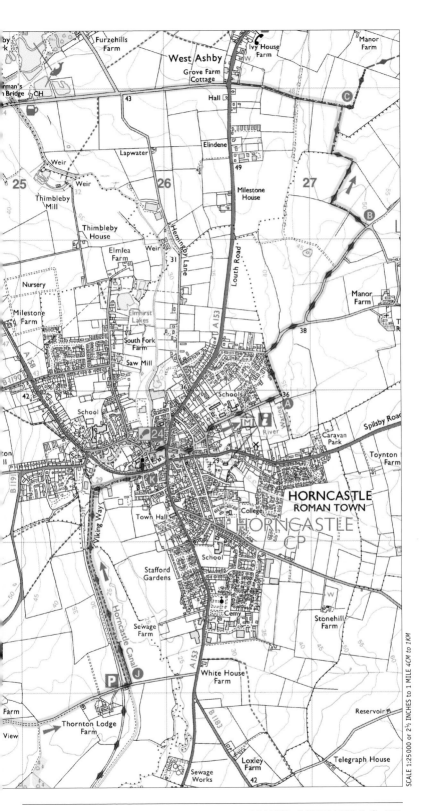

Walesby, Claxby and Normanby le Wold

Start	Walesby
Distance	6 miles (9.7km)
Approximate time	3 hours
Parking	Walesby, Village Hall
Refreshments	None
Ordnance Survey maps	Explorer 282 (Lincolnshire Wolds North), Landranger 113 (Grimsby)

This is a classic wolds walk that takes you through an open and rolling landscape of broad ridges and wide valleys, with spectacular and extensive views, particularly on the final stretch between Normanby and Walesby. It is an easy route to follow as much of it is on the Viking Way. The additional $^1/_2$ mile (800m) at the end to the 'Ramblers' Church' above Walesby is definitely worthwhile, both for the beautiful and atmospheric church itself and for the views over the wolds. The gradients are all relatively easy.

Walesby is situated at the foot of the wolds amidst some of the finest and highest scenery in Lincolnshire.

Start by turning left out of the car park to a crossroads and turn right along Moor Road. After $^1/_4$ mile (400m), turn right Ⓐ at a public byway sign, along the track to Mill House Farm and, at a fork, take the left-hand track. Go through a gate by a cattle-grid, walk along the left-hand edge of a field, go through a gate in the corner and continue uphill along the left-hand edge of the next field to a public byway post Ⓑ.

Turn left to continue along the left-hand edge of open hillside. After the next stile, the route continues along a curving track, which you follow to a T-junction. Turn right along a tarmac track to a lane Ⓒ, keep ahead and follow the lane round a right-hand bend into Claxby. Take the first lane on the left (Mulberry Road) and, when you see a public footpath sign on the right, turn left onto a grassy path, passing in front of a cottage to a gate. Go through, keep ahead to go through another gate, continue along an enclosed path and go through one more gate onto a tarmac track.

Claxby's medieval ironstone church is to the left; the route continues to the right to a T-junction Ⓓ.

Turn right along a lane and, where it bends right, keep ahead along a tarmac track (Boggle Lane). At the end of the lane, continue along an enclosed path, going through two gates, and finally walk along a track to a lane. Turn left uphill to a T-junction Ⓔ and turn right to continue up into Normanby le Wold,

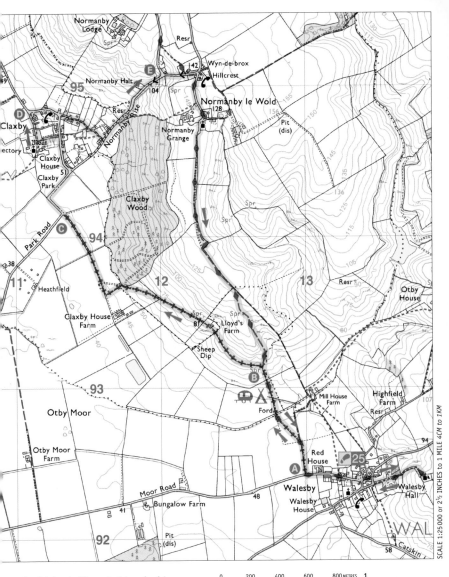

0	200	400	600	800 METRES	1

KILOMETRES
MILES

0	200	400	600 YARDS	½

the highest village in Lincolnshire. Nearby is the highest point in the county, 547ft (167m).

At a T-junction, turn right and, where the lane ends by the mainly 13th-century church, continue along a track to climb a stile. As you continue over a broad ridge along the left-hand edge of the next three fields, you enjoy superb all-round views over the rolling wolds. In the corner of the third field, follow the field edge to the right, turn left at a wall corner and keep along the left-hand field edge, heading down to a gate. Go through and, at a fork immediately in front, take the right-hand path, which continues down across the open hillside. At this point the towers of Lincoln Cathedral can be seen on the horizon. On reaching a public byway sign **B**, you rejoin the outward route and retrace your steps to Walesby.

For the extra ½ mile (800m) to Walesby Old Church (Ramblers'

Church), keep ahead at the end of Moor Road along Walesby Hill to a T-junction and turn right. Where the road bends right, turn left, at a public footpath sign to Old Church, along an enclosed tarmac track. After going through a gate, keep ahead uphill along a tree-lined track, which emerges from the trees and curves right to a gate.

Go through to reach the church, finely situated on the wolds.

It was the climb to its hilltop position that led to the church being abandoned and replaced by a new church down in the village in 1914, although it is possible that the original village occupied the slopes of the hill. The church is partly Norman, with some fine 12th-century arches in the nave. After being abandoned, it fell into disrepair but was restored in the 1930s and became a centre of pilgrimage for various local groups, including ramblers. As a result of this association, it became known as the 'Ramblers' Church', and in 1951 local ramblers donated a stained glass window depicting walkers.

From here retrace your steps downhill to the start.

Wolds near Walesby

Tealby and Kirmond le Mire

Start	Tealby
Distance	7 miles (11.3km)
Approximate time	3½ hours
Parking	Roadside parking at Tealby
Refreshments	Pubs and café at Tealby
Ordnance Survey maps	Explorer 282 (Lincolnshire Wolds North), Landranger 113 (Grimsby)

From the attractive village of Tealby, this well-waymarked route takes you across a quiet, open and rolling landscape that is typical of the Lincolnshire Wolds. Most of the way is on clear paths and tracks, and there are fine and extensive views.

The picturesque village of Tealby, situated on the lower slopes of the wolds above the little River Rase, has a thatched pub, attractive old cottages and an ironstone church that mainly dates from the 14th and 15th centuries. It was the home of the Tennyson d'Eyncourt family, who were related to Lord Tennyson, but their grand 18th-century house, Bayons Manor, was demolished in the 1960s.

The walk starts at the crossroads by the church, and the first part of it follows the well-waymarked Viking Way. Take the road signposted to North Willingham and Louth (Beck Hill). Where it bends right, keep ahead downhill along a lane and, at the bottom, cross a footbridge over the River Rase by a ford.

Keep ahead along a tarmac track which, after passing a farm on the left, winds gently uphill. Look out for where a public footpath sign directs you to turn right and continue along the right-hand edge of fields. At a field corner follow the field edge to the left, pass through a hedge gap, keep along the right-hand edge of the next field and,

after about 50 yds (46m), turn right up steps. Walk along the right-hand edge of a field, which curves left, and at the next public footpath sign turn right to continue along the left-hand edge of a field.

At a T-junction, turn left along a track and pass beside a barrier onto a road Ⓐ. Turn left and, after almost ¾ mile (1.2km), turn right through the gates of Kirmond Hall Estate Ⓑ and walk along a straight, tarmac track. Where the track bends right, keep ahead, at a public bridleway sign, to join another track, which keeps along the right-hand edge of a field. Look out for where a blue waymark directs you to bear left through a gate and follow a path gently downhill through a shallow, U-shaped valley, later keeping by a wire fence on the left.

Go through a gate in the fence, continue by the fence on the right, and the path continues in a straight line to emerge on to a lane Ⓒ. Turn left through the hamlet of Kirmond le Mire and, at a public bridleway sign, turn right along a track, passing in front of the small Victorian church. At a

Wolds near Tealby

T-junction, turn left on to a track that curves right to keep along the left-hand edge of a field. The track becomes enclosed, heads downhill between hedge banks and continues to a lane. Turn right and, after ¼ mile (400m), turn sharp left **D** at a public footpath sign, onto a path that heads across fields to a road.

Cross over, take the path ahead, which continues along the left-hand edge of a field, and in the field corner keep ahead through a hedge gap to climb a stile. Head uphill, making for the right-hand edge of trees, bear left to climb another stile and keep ahead along a track across fields. The track later keeps by the right-hand edge of woodland and, where it curves left, bear right off it and climb a stile on to a lane **E**. Keep ahead, down into a dip and up again to return to the starting point at Tealby church.

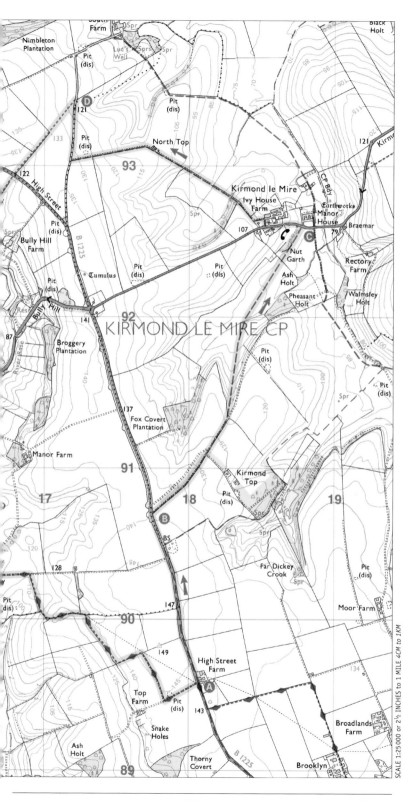

Laceby, Irby upon Humber and Aylesby

Start	Laceby
Distance	8 miles (12.9km)
Approximate time	4 hours
Parking	Laceby
Refreshments	Pubs at Laceby
Ordnance Survey maps	Explorer 284 (Grimsby, Cleethorpes & Immingham), Landranger 113 (Grimsby, Louth & Market Rasen)

This highly attractive and enjoyable walk takes you across gently rolling country on the eastern slopes of the wolds and passes though three pleasant villages, all of which have medieval churches. There are superb views both over the wolds and across the flat country to the north and east that borders the coast and Humber estuary.

Laceby is situated on the edge of the wolds just inland from the built-up area of Grimsby and Cleethorpes. The church dates mainly from the 12th and 13th centuries and has a fine 13th-century tower.

🖉 From the car park, turn right along High Street and, at a T-junction, turn right again along Caistor Road. The road bends right and later curves left to the busy A46. Cross carefully, turn left and, at a public bridleway sign, turn right Ⓐ along a tarmac track (Lopham Lane). After the last of the houses, the way continues as a rough track, which eventually emerges on to a lane. Cross the lane and the footbridge opposite and turn right Ⓑ along a track to a road.

Cross over and, at a public footpath sign Wanderlust Way, take the path opposite, which keeps by the right-hand edge of fields and above a drain. Cross a bridge over a drain, keep ahead and, in the field corner, turn left to continue along its right-hand edge. Turn right to head uphill towards a farm and turn left along a track at a T-junction, passing to the left of the farm. At the next T-junction Ⓒ, turn right – not along the track but along the parallel path that continues gently uphill along the left-hand edge of fields. The path later keeps along the left-hand, inside edge of Irby Holmes Wood and descends to emerge from the trees. Keep ahead to a public bridleway sign, turn right Ⓓ along the left-hand edge of a field and, at a T-junction, turn right to continue along the field edge, heading back towards the wood. At a waymarked post, bear left on to a path that keeps by the right-hand edge of fields. To the right are distant views of the industries of Humberside and ahead is the village

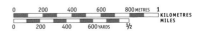

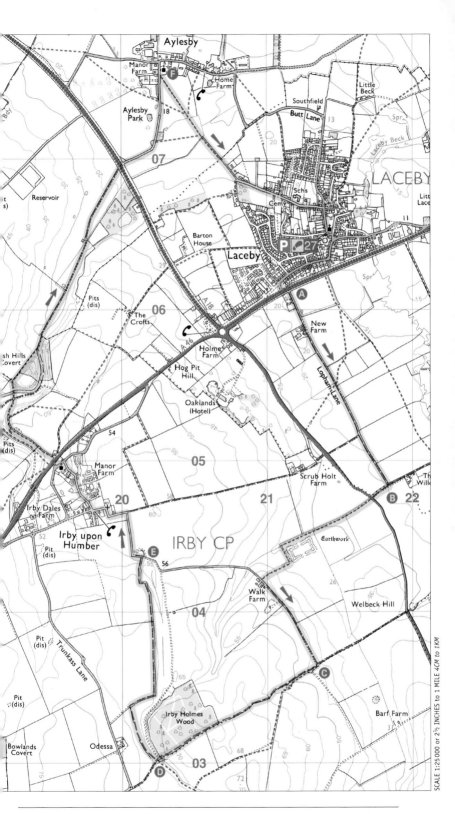

The church at Irby upon Humber

of Irby. Eventually, you head up a slight embankment and go through a hedge gap on to a lane **E**.

Turn left, follow the lane around a series of bends into Irby upon Humber – despite its name it is over 4 miles (6.4km) from the river – and at a road junction, turn right along Church Lane to the church. Apart from the tower, much of this medieval church was rebuilt during an extensive restoration in 1863. Turn left at a T-junction, turn right along a track down to the A46, turn right and, at a public footpath sign, turn left along a track beside Rowells Cottage. Turn left through a kissing-gate and turn right along the right-hand edge of a field. Now follows a delightful part of the route as you walk along a grassy path above a valley, with grand views over the rolling wolds.

The path curves right and descends. At a fork, take the right-hand path, which continues down into the valley bottom, keep ahead at a crossroads, cross a stream and head uphill, curving

right to go through a kissing-gate at the corner of woodland. Walk along the left-hand, inside edge of the wood, descending to climb a stile, turn left to emerge from the trees and bear right to continue along the edge of the wood. Go through a gate, keep along the left-hand edge of a field and continue in a straight line to go through two more gates in quick succession. Walk along an enclosed track and climb a stile on to the A18.

Cross carefully and take the narrow lane ahead (Temple Lane) into Aylesby. The church has a Perpendicular tower and is built of the local, warm-looking ironstone. Like those at Laceby and Irby, it was heavily restored in the Victorian era. Just before reaching the church, turn sharp right **F** and walk along a straight path across fields – it is a tarmac path for most of the way. After passing beside a barrier, continue along an enclosed path, which emerges on to a narrow lane.

Keep ahead, and the lane bears left into Laceby. At a T-junction, turn right to return to the start. ●

Four Lincoln Edge villages

Start	Wellingore. Shorter version starts at Navenby
Distance	9 miles (14.5km). Shorter version 6½ miles (10.5km)
Approximate time	4½ hours (3½ hours for shorter walk)
Parking	Roadside parking at Wellingore or Navenby
Refreshments	Pubs at Wellingore, pubs and café at Navenby, pubs at Coleby
Ordnance Survey maps	Explorer 272 (Lincoln), Landranger 121 (Lincoln & Newark-on-Trent)

*The four attractive villages – Wellingore, Navenby, Boothby
Graffoe and Coleby – lie along a 3-mile (4.8km) stretch of the
limestone ridge of Lincoln Edge or Cliff. The route descends from
the ridge at Navenby, continues across fields at its foot, climbs
back up to it at Coleby and then follows the Viking Way along the
ridge back to the start. From both the top and the foot of the
ridge, there are fine and extensive views. The shorter walk omits
the opening and closing section between Wellingore and Navenby.*

Start by Wellingore's medieval
church at the corner of Hall Street and
the main road and walk along the main
road away from the church. Turn left
along West Street (signposted to
Memorial Hall), turn right into
Memorial Hall Drive and, at a
T-junction, turn left to enter a playing-
field. Keep by its left-hand edge to go
through a kissing-gate and take the
path ahead across an area of scrub.

On entering a sloping field, turn right
along its top, right-hand edge and in
the corner turn right through a hedge
gap. Turn left over a stile, walk along
the top edge of the next field, climb a
stile in the corner and continue along
an enclosed path, which bends right.
Keep along the right-hand edge of a
field and turn left in the corner to
continue along its right-hand edge,
which bends right. At the next corner,
pass beside a gate onto a lane in

Navenby. At a public footpath sign,
turn left along a tarmac track called The
Smoots and, where it ends, keep ahead
along an enclosed, tree-lined path.
Follow it around a left-hand bend and,
at a public footpath sign, turn right
through a kissing-gate.

Continue along an enclosed path, go
through another kissing-gate, turn right
and almost immediately left over a stile.
Walk across a field towards Navenby
church and climb a stile onto a lane Ⓐ.

*If starting the walk at Navenby, walk
down Church Lane from the main road
to pick up the full walk here.*

Turn left downhill, follow the lane
around right- and left-hand bends,
cross a bridge over a disused railway
line and, after 1 mile (1.6km), turn right
Ⓑ along a straight, hedge-lined track.
Later keep along the left-hand edge of
fields, follow the track around right-
and left-hand bends and continue to a

narrow lane **C**. Turn left and, after nearly 1 mile (1.6km), turn right at a public footpath sign in front of a house **D**. As you walk along the left-hand edge of a field, glimpses of Somerton Castle can be seen over to the left. The castle was built in 1281 by a bishop of Durham but only a tower survives from this medieval building, incorporated into the present 17th-century farmhouse.

Turn right in the field corner to continue along its left-hand edge, cross a footbridge over a ditch and keep ahead along an enclosed track. The track bends left to continue across fields and, where it turns left again, turn right along the right-hand field edge. Cross a plank footbridge, walk along the right-hand edge of the next field and, at a waymarked post, turn left to continue along the right-hand edge. To the right are fine views of the tower and spire of Coleby church on top of the edge.

The path widens into a track that continues to a lane. Turn right, cross a bridge over the disused railway again and head up the edge or cliff into Coleby. At a public footpath sign by the village green, turn left by the pub to see the fine medieval church, parts of which date back to the 11th century. Otherwise, turn right **E** along a narrow, enclosed path, here rejoining the Viking

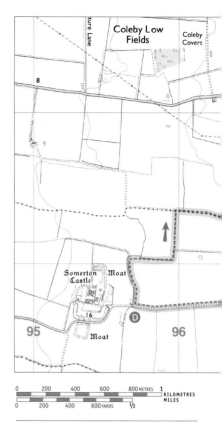

A distant view of Coleby church on Lincoln Edge

Way for the rest of the route.

The path twists and turns, turning right at one point to a stile. Climb it and continue along the top, left-hand edge of a series of sloping fields and over a succession of stiles, eventually turning left over a stile and heading diagonally across a field. Climb a stile in the corner and continue along a lane through Boothby Graffoe. Where it bends left just before the 19th-century church, keep ahead **F** along a track to a stile. After climbing it, keep along the top left-hand edge of fields again, later continuing along an enclosed path.

Follow this path around left- and right-hand bends to emerge, via a kissing-gate and steps, on to a lane in Navenby. Turn left, turn right along an enclosed tarmac path (Cat Walk) towards the church, and the path bends first left and then right to emerge onto a lane by the church. This impressive

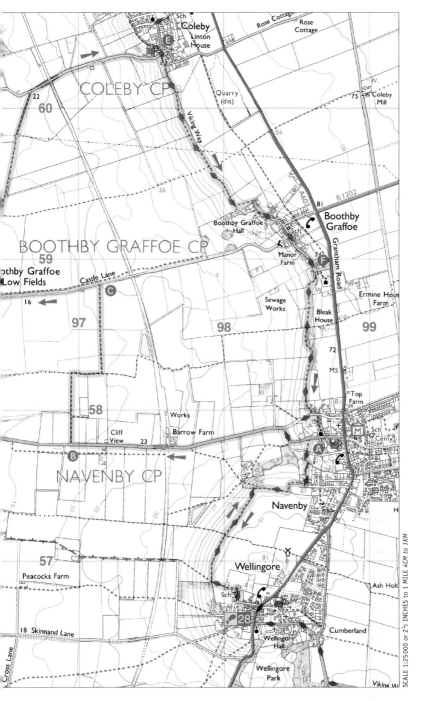

building dates mainly from the 14th and 15th centuries but was heavily restored in the Victorian era. The west tower was rebuilt in the 18th century after its predecessor collapsed.

Turn left to the start if you began the walk at Navenby. To return to the start of the full walk, turn right past the church and, at a public footpath sign, turn left over a stile Ⓐ. Here you rejoin the outward route and retrace your steps to Wellingore.

Further Information

 ### The National Trust

Anyone who likes visiting places of natural beauty and/or historic interest has cause to be grateful to the National Trust. Without it, many such places would probably have vanished by now.

It was in response to the pressures on the countryside posed by the relentless march of Victorian industrialisation that the trust was set up in 1895. Its founders, inspired by the common goals of protecting and conserving Britain's national heritage and widening public access to it, were Sir Robert Hunter, Octavia Hill and Canon Rawnsley: respectively a solicitor, a social reformer and a clergyman. The latter was particularly influential. As a canon of Carlisle Cathedral and vicar of Crosthwaite (near Keswick), he was concerned about threats to the Lake District and had already been active in protecting footpaths and promoting public access to open countryside. After the flooding of Thirlmere in 1879 to create a large reservoir, he became increasingly convinced that the only effective way to guarantee protection was outright ownership of land.

The purpose of the National Trust is to preserve areas of natural beauty and sites of historic interest by acquisition, holding them in trust for the nation and making them available for public access and enjoyment. Some of its properties have been acquired through purchase, but many of the Trust's properties have been donated. Nowadays it is not only one of the biggest landowners in the country, but also one of the most active conservation charities, protecting 581,113 acres (253,176 ha) of land, including 555 miles (892km) of coastline, and over 300 historic properties in England, Wales and Northern Ireland. (There is a separate National Trust for Scotland, which was set up in 1931.)

Furthermore, once a piece of land has come under National Trust ownership, it is difficult for its status to be altered. As a result of parliamentary legislation in 1907, the Trust was given the right to declare its property inalienable, so ensuring that in any subsequent dispute it can appeal directly to parliament.

As it works towards its dual aims of conserving areas of attractive countryside and encouraging greater public access (not easy to reconcile in this age of mass tourism), the Trust provides an excellent service for walkers by creating new concessionary paths and waymarked trails, maintaining stiles and foot bridges and combating the ever-increasing problem of footpath erosion.

For details of membership, contact the National Trust at the address on page 94.

 ### The Ramblers' Association

No organisation works more actively to protect and extend the rights and interests of walkers in the countryside than the Ramblers' Association. Its aims are clear: to foster a greater knowledge, love and care of the countryside; to assist in the protection and enhancement of public rights of way and areas of natural beauty; to work for greater public access to the countryside; and to encourage more people to take up rambling as a healthy, recreational leisure activity.

It was founded in 1935 when, following the setting up of a National Council of Ramblers' Federations in 1931, a number of federations earlier formed in London, Manchester, the Midlands and elsewhere came together to create a more effective pressure group, to deal with such problems as the disappearance and obstruction of footpaths, the prevention of access to open mountain and moorland and increasing hostility from landowners. This was the era of the mass trespasses, when there were sometimes violent

The Grantham Canal

confrontations between ramblers and gamekeepers, especially on the moorlands of the Peak District.

Since then the Ramblers' Association has played an influential role in preserving and developing the national footpath network, supporting the creation of national parks and encouraging the designation and waymarking of long-distance routes.

Our freedom to walk in the countryside is precarious and requires constant vigilance. As well as the perennial problems of footpaths being illegally obstructed, disappearing through lack of use or extinguished by housing or road construction, new dangers can spring up at any time.

It is to meet such problems and dangers that the Ramblers' Association exists and represents the interests of all walkers. The address to write to for information on the Ramblers' Association and how to become a member is given on page 95.

 ### Walkers and the Law

The average walker in a national park or other popular walking area, armed with the appropriate Ordnance Survey map, reinforced perhaps by a guidebook giving detailed walking instructions, is unlikely to run into legal difficulties, but it is useful to know something about the law relating to public rights of way. The right to walk over certain parts of the countryside has developed over a long period, and how such rights came into being is a complex subject, too lengthy to be discussed here. The following comments are intended simply as a helpful guide, backed up by the Countryside Access Charter, a concise summary of walkers' rights and obligations drawn up by the Countryside Agency (see page 94).

Basically there are two main kinds of public rights of way: footpaths (for walkers only) and bridleways (for walkers, riders on horseback and pedal cyclists). Footpaths and bridleways are shown by broken green lines on Ordnance Survey Pathfinder and Outdoor Leisure maps and broken red lines on Landranger maps. There is also a third category, called byways: chiefly broad tracks (green lanes) or farm roads, which walkers, riders and cyclists have to share, usually only occasionally, with motor vehicles. Many of these public paths have been in existence for hundreds of years and some

Countryside Access Charter

Your rights of way are:

- public footpaths – on foot only. Sometimes waymarked in yellow
- bridleways – on foot, horseback and pedal cycle. Sometimes waymarked in blue
- byways (usually old roads), most 'roads used as public paths' and, of course, public roads – all traffic has the right of way

Use maps, signs and waymarks to check rights of way. Ordnance Survey Pathfinder and Landranger maps show most public rights of way

On rights of way you can:

- take a pram, pushchair or wheelchair if practicable
- take a dog (on a lead or under close control)
- take a short route round an illegal obstruction or remove it sufficiently to get past

You have a right to go for recreation to:

- public parks and open spaces – on foot
- most commons near older towns and cities – on foot and sometimes on horseback
- private land where the owner has a formal agreement with the local authority

In addition you can use the following by local or established custom or consent, but ask for advice if you are unsure:

- many areas of open country, such as moorland, fell and coastal areas, especially those in the care of the National Trust, and some commons
- some woods and forests, especially those owned by the Forestry Commission
- country parks and picnic sites
- most beaches
- canal towpaths
- some private paths and tracks Consent sometimes extends to horse-riding and cycling

For your information:

- county councils and London boroughs maintain and record rights of way, and register commons
- obstructions, dangerous animals, harassment and misleading signs on rights of way are illegal and you should report them to the county council
- paths across fields can be ploughed, but must normally be reinstated within two weeks
- landowners can require you to leave land to which you have no right of access
- motor vehicles are normally permitted only on roads, byways and some 'roads used as public paths'

even originated as prehistoric trackways and have been in constant use for well over 2,000 years. Ways known as RUPPs (roads used as public paths) still appear on some maps. The legal definition of such byways is ambiguous and they are gradually being reclassified as footpaths, bridleways or byways.

The term 'right of way' means exactly what it says. It gives right of passage over what, in the vast majority of cases, is private land, and you are required to keep to the line of the path and not stray on to the land on either side. If you inadvertently wander off the right of way – either because of faulty map-reading or because the route is not clearly indicated on the ground – you are technically trespassing

and the wisest course is to ask the nearest available person (farmer or fellow walker) to direct you back to the correct route. There are stories about unpleasant confrontations between walkers and farmers at times, but in general most farmers are co-operative when responding to a genuine and polite request for assistance in route-finding.

Obstructions can sometimes be a problem and probably the most common of these is where a path across a field has been ploughed up. It is legal for a farmer to plough up a path provided that he restores it within two weeks, barring exceptionally bad weather. This does not always happen and here the walker is presented with a dilemma: to follow the line of the path, even if this inevitably means treading on crops, or to walk around the edge of the field. The latter course of action often seems the best but this means that you would be trespassing and not keeping to the exact line of the path. In the case of other obstructions which may block a path (illegal fences and locked gates etc), common sense has to be used in order to negotiate them by the easiest method – detour or removal. You should only ever remove as much as is necessary to get through, and if you can easily go round the obstruction without causing any damage, then you should do so. If you have any problems negotiating rights of way, you should report the matter to the rights of way department of the relevant council, which will take action with the landowner concerned.

Apart from rights of way enshrined by law, there are a number of other paths available to walkers. Permissive or concessionary paths have been created where a landowner has given permission for the public to use a particular route across his land. The main problem with these is that, as they have been granted as a concession, there is no legal right to use them and therefore they can be extinguished at any time. In practice, many of these concessionary routes have been established on land owned either by large public bodies such as the Forestry Commission, or by a private one, such as the National Trust, and as these mainly encourage walkers to use their paths, they are unlikely to be closed unless a change of ownership occurs.

Walkers also have free access to country parks (except where requested to keep away from certain areas for ecological reasons, e.g wildlife protection, woodland regeneration, etc), canal towpaths and most beaches. By custom, though not by right, you are generally free to walk across the open and uncultivated higher land of mountain, moorland and fell, but this varies from area to area and from one season to another – grouse moors, for example, will be out of bounds during the breeding and shooting seasons and some open areas are used as Ministry of Defence firing ranges, for which reason access will be restricted. In some areas the situation has been clarified as a result of 'access agreements' between the landowners and either the county council or the national park authority, which clearly define when and where you can walk over such open country.

 ### Walking Safety

Although the reasonably gentle countryside that is the subject of this book offers no real dangers to walkers at any time of the year, it is still advisable to take sensible precautions and follow certain well-tried guidelines.

Always take with you both warm and waterproof clothing and sufficient food and drink. Wear suitable footwear, i.e. strong walking boots or shoes that give a good grip over stony ground, on slippery

Tattershall Castle

The Humber Bridge – the world's third-longest single-span suspension bridge

slopes and in muddy conditions. Try to obtain a local weather forecast and bear it in mind before you start. Do not be afraid to abandon your proposed route and return to your starting point in the event of a sudden and unexpected deterioration in the weather.

All the walks described in this book will be safe to do, given due care and respect, even during the winter. Indeed, a crisp, fine winter day often provides perfect walking conditions, with firm ground underfoot and a clarity unique to this time of the year. The most difficult hazard likely to be encountered is mud, especially when walking along woodland and field paths, farm tracks and bridleways – the latter in particular can often get churned up by cyclists and horses. In summer, an additional difficulty may be narrow and overgrown paths, particularly along the edges of cultivated fields. Neither should constitute a major problem provided that the appropriate footwear is worn.

Useful Organisations

Council for the Protection of Rural England
25 Buckingham Palace Road,
London SW1W 0PP.
Tel. 020 7976 6433

Countryside Agency
John Dower House,
Crescent Place, Cheltenham,
Gloucestershire GL50 3RA.
Tel. 01242 521381

Forestry Commission
Information Branch,
231 Corstorphine Road,
Edinburgh EH12 7AT.
Tel. 0131 334 0303

Lincolnshire County Council
County Offices, Newland,
Lincoln LN1 1YG.
Tel. 01522 552222;
Fax 01522 552288

Long Distance Walkers' Association
Bank House, High Street, Wrotham,
Sevenoaks, Kent TN15 7AE.
Tel. 01732 883705

National Trust
Membership and general enquiries:
PO Box 39, Bromley,
Kent BR1 3XL.
Tel. 020 8315 1111
E-mail: enquiries@ntrust.org.uk
East Midlands Regional Office:
Clumber Park Stableyard,
Worksop, Nottinghamshire S80 3BE.
Tel. 01909 486411; Fax 01909 486377

North-East Lincolnshire Council
Civic Offices, Knoll Street,
Cleethorpes, N.E. Lincs. DN35 8LN.
Tel. 01472 324468; Fax 01472 324502

North Lincolnshire Council
Countryside Team. Tel. 01724 297387

Ordnance Survey
Romsey Road, Maybush,
Southampton SO16 4GU.
Tel. 08456 05 05 05 (Lo-call)

Ramblers' Association
2nd Floor, Camelford House,
87–90 Albert Embankment,
London SE1 7TW.
Tel. 020 7339 8500

Tourist information:
East Midlands Tourist Board
Exchequergate, Lincoln LN2 1PZ.
Tel. 01522 531521; Fax 01522 532501
Lincolnshire Tourism: 01522 526450
*Local tourist information centres (*not
open all year):*
*Alford: 01507 462143
Boston: 01205 356656
Brigg: 01652 657053
Chapel St Leonards: 01754 872415
Gainsborough: 01427 615411

Grantham: 01476 406166
Grimsby: 01472 342422
*Horncastle: 01507 526636
Lincoln: 01522 873213/873256
Louth: 01507 609289
Mablethorpe: 01507 474939
Scunthorpe: 01724 297354
Skegness: 01754 764821
Sleaford: 01529 414294
Spalding: 01775 725468
Stamford: 01780 755611
*Woodhall Spa: 01526 353775

Youth Hostels Association
Trevelyan House, Dimple Road,
Matlock, Derbyshire, DE4 3YH.
Tel. 01629 592600
website: www.yha.org.uk

Ordnance Survey Maps of Lincolnshire

The area of Lincolnshire is covered by
Ordnance Survey 1:50 000 ($1^{1}/_{4}$ inches to
1 mile or 2cm to 1km) scale Landranger
map sheets 112, 113, 120, 121, 122, 129,
130, and 131. These all-purpose maps are
packed with information to help you
explore the area and show viewpoints,
picnic sites, places of interest and caravan
and camping sites.

To examine the area in more detail and
especially if you are planning walks,
Ordnance Survey Explorer maps at
1:25 000 ($2^{1}/_{2}$ inches to 1 mile or 4cm to
1km) scale are ideal:

234	235	247	248	249
261	272	273	274	280
281	282	283	284	

To get to the Lincolnshire area use the
Ordnance Survey Routeplanner Map Great
Britain 2002 at 1:625 000 (1 inch to 10
miles or 4cm to 25km) scale or Road Map
5 (East Midlands and East Anglia
including London) or Road Map 8 (South
East England including London) at
1:250 000 (1 inch to 4 miles or 1cm to
2.5km) scale.

Ordnance Survey maps are available
from most booksellers, stationers and
newsagents.

Lincoln Cathedral

Index

Entries in *italic type* refer to illustrations